MW01048470

Willow Run

Willow Run

Wally Wiggins

GAMMA BOOKS
ITHACA, NEW YORK

www.wallywiggins.com

Photographs by author
Book design by Mary A. Scott

Library of Congress Catalog Card Number: 99-62307

ISBN 0-933124-03-1

Printed in the United States of America
First printing

To Joyce . . .
Kaethe, Marcus, Scott and Jonni

Chapter One

THE VILLAGE OF GLENWOOD LAND-
ing is a small town nestled at the headwaters of Lake Iroquois. Most people refer to the village as Glenwood since
the "landing" is as obsolete as the *Iroquois Queen*, a pad-
dle-wheeler that picked up and discharged her passengers
there until the turn of the century. A distinguished university that is sprawled across the hillside above the lake
brings economic stability and an air of sophistication to the
picturesque upstate community.

Michael O'Leary is one of a handful of attorneys who
maintains his office in the shadow of the county courthouse. After graduating from law school he hung out his
shingle in the village, and during the twenty years that followed he earned a reputation as a good lawyer and an
honorable man.

As he began to open his mail on a cold day in early
December, his secretary called him on the intercom.

"A young woman would like to speak with you about a personal matter, Mr. O'Leary. Shall I bring her back to your office?"

"Sure," Michael replied, putting his mail aside and clearing a pile of books off the chair reserved for his clients. Seconds later the young woman was ushered into his office. Michael stood up as she entered and gestured for her to sit down across from his desk. As the secretary closed the door behind her, Michael settled into his high-back swivel chair.

"My name is Rhonda Fleming," the young woman began. Michael slid his glasses down and looked over their rims directly into her startling green eyes.

"How can I help you?" he asked.

"I need to ask you some questions about the law."

"You've come to the right place," Michael said affably.

"Do you mind if I record our conversation? I want to make a tape of what you say to me so I can study it later. Is that all right?" she asked.

"That's okay. I'm paid by the hour, you know. It's all the same to me."

"First, I want you to tell me all there is to know about privileged communications. I understand that if I am your client, everything we say to each other is privileged, is that correct?"

"For the most part that's true. Of course there are always exceptions."

"Like what?"

"Well, if you were to tell me something while my secretary was in the room, it would not be privileged. The privilege only applies to those matters we discuss in absolute privacy."

"I see. And are there other exceptions?"

"I suppose if you told me that just before you came to my office you had planted a bomb in the nursery school building down the street, I would have some trouble keeping that to myself," Michael replied. "So what is this all about?"

She sat back in her chair, paused thoughtfully, and said, "I want you to teach me about murder."

"How to prevent it or perpetrate it?" Michael smiled.

"How to commit it without going to jail," she answered solemnly.

Michael leaned forward in his chair. "I think this consultation has just come to an end. You may be joking but I can't be sure, and I am unwilling to take a chance."

"Can we talk about it?"

"Of course we can talk about it. You just can't act on it."

"What is the difference between murder and manslaughter?"

"About twenty years in jail."

"I don't mean the penalty, I mean the definition."

"I knew what you meant, Ms. Fleming, I only wanted to lighten the conversation a little," Michael said, standing up and walking over to the bookshelves that lined his office wall. He pulled down a thin black volume, flipped a few pages and began to read, "A person is guilty of murder in the second degree when: With intent to cause the death of another person, he causes the death of such person or of a third person."

"That's all of it?" she demanded.

"Not exactly. The statute goes on to describe the defense of extreme emotional distress."

"If the killer commits the crime under extreme emotional distress does he get off scot-free?"

"No ma'am, the charge just drops to manslaughter and the sentence is reduced accordingly."

"How much?"

"Well, that depends on the judge, I'd say. The minimum sentence could be as little as 8⅓ years."

Ms. Fleming stood up and said, "I think that's all I need to know for now. How much do I owe you?"

Michael glanced at the grandfather clock on the far wall of his office. "I guess twenty-five dollars ought to do it."

She reached in her purse and put the money on his desk. "Thank you," she said, then turned and walked briskly from his office.

"I'll be damned," Michael exclaimed, picking up the bills and stuffing them in his pocket.

That night Doc Stuart came by Michael's home to play chess, as he had done several evenings each month for many years. Doc had been practicing medicine in Glenwood for as long as Michael had been separating people from their money in the courtroom. They had been good friends in high school and renewed the friendship when Doc returned to Glenwood to join his father in general practice. He was best man at Michael's wedding, and after Doc married Beth the two families became inseparable. When Michael's wife died, Beth became a surrogate mother for Michael's two children.

As Michael was mixing their drinks after their chess game, he said, "Do you ever wonder what happens to your patients in the end?"

"You mean how they die?"

"No, no. What I'm talking about for instance . . . there was a young lady who came to see me at the office this morning. I sure would like to know what *her* story is."

"How come?"

"Well, it sounded as if she wanted to kill somebody and avoid going to jail. I really don't think she was serious about it, but it's been bothering me. The thing is that with most of my clients, I rarely find out what happens in the third act. I wonder about it most often when I'm successful in getting an acquittal in a criminal matter, or when I win a custody case. You must have the same situation, I mean some kid comes in to you with a bullet in his foot. You take a medical history but you don't get the whole story. Did the guy who shot him get arrested? Was it self-defense or did he shoot himself in the foot?"

"I don't think about that, don't you see," the doctor answered, leaning back in the familiar overstuffed chair. "I'm a physician. I'm only interested in knowing how the foot turns out after I finish treating him."

"At least once in a while you must be curious how the story ends."

"Oh, I suppose so, but unless I'm certain it's going to turn out okay, I guess I don't want to know about it," he shrugged.

"But that's not what the real world is all about."

"I see tragedy every day of my life in the *real* world, Mike. I don't need to go looking for it."

"Some of the greatest books are—"

"I don't need them. I give them all to you, old buddy. At the end of the day I don't want to contemplate anything more complex than Monday Night Football or our regular chess games, where it doesn't really matter who wins or loses."

"Don't try to tell me that you didn't try to win tonight . . . and every other night we've played during the past twenty years."

"Of course I tried to win, and I would have if you hadn't snuck up behind me like you usually do. What I meant was, after the game is over it doesn't really matter to me who won or lost. Life is different. It's not a game, it's serious business. Given a choice between *Death of a Salesman* and *My Fair Lady*, I'd rather dance all night. Which reminds me," he said, glancing at his watch, "I've got rounds at the hospital tomorrow morning at 7:30. It's time I stopped dancing for the night."

"Before you go, I've got a favor to ask," Michael said hesitantly. "I've written a couple of short stories and I was wondering if you might be willing to read one of them? I'd like you to tell me what you think."

"Is this what that last conversation was all about? You snuck up on me again, didn't you?"

"Not really. They are only short stories based on what I've seen and heard and done right here in Glenwood."

"Did you write them just for fun, or what?"

"Honestly, Doc? I'm not sure. I guess that's the reason I want you to read them. If my best friend thinks they're worthless . . ." Michael shrugged his shoulders.

"I think it's a dangerous business," Doc said, easing himself out of his chair. "What do I know about such things? It would be much better if you ask someone who has some professional experience in the field. I'm just an overworked general practitioner who reads the *Glenwood Gazette, The Sunday Times* and *The New England Journal of Medicine.* I started to read a novel two months ago and I still haven't finished it. I may never find out how it ends, unless they make it into a movie."

"It's only a short story . . . ten or twelve pages."

"Okay, so what's it all about? Is it a murder mystery involving that new client of yours?"

"No, nothing as exciting as that. As a matter of fact, it's a true story. Happened when Judge McDougal was still on the bench."

"Good Lord, Ed McDougal has been dead almost twenty years."

"You're right, this goes back to the year I opened my office." Michael walked over to his desk and picked up a dozen sheets of paper and handed them to the doctor. Doc glanced at the title.

"*Jack O' Hearts*. Okay, I'll give it a shot," he said, folding the pages and slipping them into his pocket. "But you should really give it to Beth, she would love to read it."

"Maybe next time. . . . I want you to read the first one. It's part of the price you pay for being my best friend."

"You should have told me that in the first place," Doc said, taking his heavy winter coat down from the wooden peg in the front hallway. "We'll get together over the weekend, God willing and the well don't run dry," he added, as he let himself out the front door.

 # Chapter Two

The Jack O' Hearts

Honorable Edward J. McDougal scanned the accusatory instrument charging Jack Moynahan with the crime of destroying government property.

"Now what have you done, you old scoundrel?" Judge McDougal thought as he picked up the roster of lawyers practicing in his court. He ran his finger down the list until he saw Michael O'Leary's name.

"With Kevin Hanrahan prosecuting we might as well make this an all-Irish affair," the judge said to himself. He picked up the phone and dialed the number opposite O'Leary's name.

"Law Office."

"Sure, and is this Michael O'Leary himself?" Judge McDougal demanded.

"That's just right sir, and who do I have the pleasure of speaking to?" I asked.

"It's Judge McDougal here and I'm wondering, Mr. O'Leary, as the newest member of our local bar, if you have the time to help out the court in a bit of a criminal case that's before me?"

"Oh good morning sir. But of course I'd consider it an honor to appear in your court, Judge McDougal. And would you be telling me what kind of a case it is, sir?"

"Well, you understand I don't know the merits of the matter, but old Jack Moynahan got himself charged with destroying government property. I was thinking you might like to look into it, as a favor to the court you might say. He's been arraigned before me, pleaded not guilty and says he wants a jury trial. He's entitled to a lawyer but he hasn't a nickel to his name. Never has had, as long as I can remember. I've set the case down for trial next week. We'll pick a jury on Monday morning at 9:30 sharp."

"Yes sir, I'll be there," I said enthusiastically. I opened my appointment book with the name Michael O'Leary, Esq. embossed in gold in the lower right hand corner along with the words "Compliments of Lawyers Publishing Co." "Let's see now, Monday, August 6," I mumbled to myself as I flipped the pages. "I guess I can make that okay," I said aloud, staring at all the empty pages in my book.

My office was located right on State Street in the center of town, which consisted of four blocks east and west and three blocks north and south. A jewelry store occupied the first floor, a young insurance agent rented the front office on the second floor and my office was down the hall in the rear, with a view of the back entrance to the local pool hall.

I hung the "Back in 10 minutes" sign on the handle of the front door and hurried over to police headquarters to examine the complaint filed against my new client. On the way I wondered why I hadn't heard about the case, since Glenwood was a pretty small town, with a limited amount of government property to be destroyed.

Sergeant Collins was on the desk when I entered the office.

"Hey Red," he said, continuing to peck away with his two index fingers on his Smith Corona manual typewriter. His hands were badly gnarled by arthritis but he could keep that old machine smoking.

"What say, Sergeant? . . . Got a minute?" I asked.

He nodded, turning his head sideways to avoid the smoke from the cigarette that perpetually dangled from his lips. When he finished the line he was typing, he leaned back in his chair and smiled up at me.

"What can I do for you, Counselor?" he asked.

"I need to take a look at the accusatory on Jack Moynahan. Judge McDougal has assigned me to defend him," I said with a touch of pride in my voice.

"Oh ho," he said as he shuffled through a stack of papers on his desk. "You got your work cut out for you on this one, Red. You're dealing with government property here."

He slid the affidavit across the counter and I began to read the details of the crime my client was accused of.

Jess Parker, being duly sworn, deposes and says: That on the 14th day of July 1979 deponent was called to Cell Block A on the second floor of the county jail on the complaint of Sidney Rothenberg, a prisoner incarcerated therein. Prisoner Rothenberg claimed that the floor of his cell was flooded from a leak which was coming from the adjoining cell. I investi-

gated and discovered that the water was coming from the toilet in the cell occupied by Jack Moynahan. Upon further investigation I found that Prisoner Moynahan had kicked and broken the toilet bowl and I reported the matter to the sheriff.

(signed) Jess Parker, Deputy

Sergeant Collins smiled as he watched me reading the affidavit.

"So what do you think, Counselor?" he said.

"Innocent until proved guilty beyond a reasonable doubt, that's all I've got to say," I replied, leaving the office before he had a chance to say anything further.

My next stop was the county jail to visit the defendant Jack Moynahan, whose criminal stature in my view had been dramatically diminished by the nature of the crime. When I entered the sheriff's office, which was connected to the county jail, the sheriff himself was standing behind the counter.

"Can I help you?" he asked in a real friendly way.

"Yes sir. My name is Michael O'Leary. Judge McDougal has assigned me to defend Jack Moynahan, and I'd like to talk to him if I may."

The sheriff held out his hand. "I'm Sheriff Williams. You must be Sean O'Leary's boy, am I right?" he said, shaking my hand with a firm grip.

"Yes sir, Sean is my dad. I didn't know you knew him."

"Why sure. Your old man and I used to bum around together years back. Now who is it you want to see?"

"Jack Moynahan," I said sheepishly.

"Oh yes, old Jack Moynahan," he replied.

"Are you sure he did it, Sheriff?" I asked.

"Of course I'm sure; otherwise I wouldn't have charged him now, would I?"

"Well I still want to see him, Sheriff. I mean I'm assigned to defend him, not to judge him. That will be for a jury to decide."

"Don't tell me that you are going to put us to the expense of trying that old drunk! The case is open and shut."

"Did anybody see him do it?"

"Don't matter. You put a man in a single cell with a toilet which is working just fine, and within a few days after he's in there, there's a crack in the toilet bowl that wasn't there when we put him in. He's guilty as hell. He knows he done it, but now he's got a lawyer I suppose we'll have to spend all kinds of taxpayer money to prove it— Oh well, go on up to the attorney's room and I'll send him over."

The conversation with the sheriff had unnerved me. I began to think it might be best for everyone if I just had him plead guilty. After all, I wasn't going to get paid, and for sure this case wasn't going to be the one that catapulted me to stardom.

When Jack Moynahan shuffled into the attorney's room I was flabbergasted. He was the spitting image of my Grandpa Branigan. He stood no more than five-foot-two inches tall and didn't weigh more than a bucket of beer. His right eye was partially closed and clouded over, but he had the most engaging grin I'd ever seen, with one gold tooth up and one gold tooth down.

"Jack Moynahan is me name," he said, offering his wrinkled hand to me.

"I'm Michael O'Leary. Pleased to meet you." We shook hands and sat down across from each other at an old wooden table scarred with cigarette burns laid down over the years by the prisoners and their attorneys. I offered him a smoke. He accepted it eagerly and we both lit up.

"Sheriff said my attorney was here and wanted to see me, but you ain't old enough to be a real lawyer, are yeh?"

"Well sir, I've been assigned by Judge McDougal to defend you on a charge of destroying government property," I replied solemnly, ignoring his question about my age.

"By Christ there's no way in 'ell they kin prove I busted that leaky shitter," he exclaimed.

I was encouraged. Perhaps he was innocent. This was my first criminal case and I desperately wanted him to be innocent. Besides, there was no way I was going to let a jury convict someone who looked just like my Grandpa Branigan.

"I've got some questions I must ask you, Mr. Moynahan," I said in my most lawyer-like voice, as I removed my yellow legal pad from the vinyl briefcase my mother gave me when I graduated from law school. Moynahan took a deep drag on his cigarette and squinted through his one good eye. He let the smoke seep out of his mouth and into his nose.

"Now before you say anything, Mr. Moynahan, I want you to know that you and I have a lawyer-client relationship. Anything you say to me is strictly confidential," I said earnestly.

Moynahan put his elbows on the table and leaned forward conspiratorially, "The D.A. got this room bugged, ye know," he whispered.

"That's impossible."

"Oh it tis, hey? Then how come when Hokey Terwilleger got hisself arrested for assault, and he told his lawyer in this very room that the only way he could pay his fee was from the money what he stole from Smitty's gas station, they charged him with burglarizing the gas station the very next day? Tell me that, will yeh?" he demanded.

I didn't know how to answer that exactly, so I just leaned close to him and whispered, "I'm only going to ask you one question, Mr. Moynahan, but you have to swear to tell me the truth."

"I swear on the blood of Jaysus, Joseph and Mary," he hissed.

I looked at the notes I had taken at the police station from the accusatory affidavit, glanced around the tiny room to see where the bug might be hidden and then whispered, "Did you on the 14th day of July 1979 break the toilet in your cell by kicking it with your boot, as it says here in the accusatory instrument?"

Moynahan stood up slowly, placed his hand over his heart and declared, "I swear on the soul o' me dear dead mother, that I, Jack Mulligan Moynahan, never, never on the 14th day of July 1979, or any other day, broke the damn toilet by kicking it with me boot, amen, so help me God and may the good Lord strike me dead on this very spot if I'm not tellin' the truth." He sat down in his chair, crossed his arms over his chest and said, "Further, the defendant sayeth not."

I glowed. Maybe it wasn't exactly the case I had in mind, and maybe Mr. Moynahan's acquittal wouldn't hit the front pages of the local paper, but I had myself a real live innocent client and I would defend him with every ounce of skill I possessed. We shook hands and I gave him my pack of cigarettes. "I'll see you in court on Monday, Mr. Moynahan," I said, as I pushed the buzzer to signal the sheriff to come and unlock the door that imprisoned us in the attorney's room.

As he was leaving, Jack turned back to me, "And the truth shall set me free," he said as he was led back to his cell.

I went directly to my office and spent the afternoon doing legal research, but I couldn't find a single precedent involving broken jail toilets. This was a clear case of circumstantial evidence.

That evening when I returned to my apartment I spent an hour studying the toilet in the bathroom. I kicked it with rubber boots, work boots and ski boots. I kicked it with the toe and the heel. I kicked it with my left foot and my right. I couldn't make a dent in it. Obviously my client was telling me the truth. There was no way Mr. Moynahan could have broken that toilet. However, since the sheriff had referred to my client as "an old drunk," I decided to check his criminal record. I discovered to my horror that he had twenty-three prior convictions for being drunk and disorderly.

The day of the trial was a scorcher. The overhead fans turned lazily in the antiquated courtroom. The windows were all wide open, allowing the sounds of the village to intermingle with the judicial proceedings. I was champing at the bit to pick my first jury. Since Mr. Moynahan hadn't inquired as to my courtroom experience I didn't volunteer the information that I had never tried a case before. I was managing the jury picking process without stumbling too badly until I reached Mrs. Salvatore. My exact words to her were, "Now tell me, please, Mrs. Salvatore, are you the mother of the beautiful Anna Salvatore, who goes to the Church of the Sacred Heart where I was an altar boy for five years?"

The judge sustained the prosecutor's objection with a bit of a smile and suggested that I move on to a different line of questioning. I asked each juror if it would make any difference to them if Mr. Moynahan decided not to take the stand and testify, explaining to them that he did not have an obligation to do so and that Judge McDougal would tell them straight out that they must not consider his failure to testify as evidence of guilt. When I asked one of the jurors, Mrs. Cunningham, about that she said, "Well if he's innocent like you claim, I don't understand why he wouldn't want to say so." Then she turned to Judge McDougal and demanded, "Is he telling it right, Judge? Is that the way it is?" and Judge McDougal replied, "That's the way it is, Effie, that's the law." "Sounds like a dumb law to me, Ed," she answered. I dismissed her from the jury, and she stamped out of the courtroom like she had been insulted. In any event, we ended up with two women and four men on the jury and they all promised me that they wouldn't convict Mr. Moynahan unless they were satisfied beyond a reasonable doubt that he was guilty.

The prosecutor only put on one witness and that was Jess Parker, the deputy sheriff who was on duty at the time Jack Moynahan was put in his cell. Jess testified that when he locked Mr. Moynahan up, the toilet was working just fine with no sign of a crack anywhere. But after the second day when he investigated the cause of the water leaking all over the floor, he discovered this big crack in the side of the bowl where Moynahan had kicked it and broken it.

When it came time for me to cross-examine Jess I was pretty nervous because of my lack of experience. I said, "Now Mr. Parker, you don't really believe Mr. Moynahan broke that toilet, do you?"

"Of course I do. Everybody knows Moynahan did it," he replied indignantly.

"Did you see him do it?" I asked.

"No, I didn't see him do it. But that don't mean he didn't do it," Jess said with his jaw stuck out belligerently.

"And you claim, do you, that Mr. Moynahan was the only one who could have done it?"

"There weren't nobody else in there but him in that cell. He was there all by hisself so that kinda proves it, don't it?"

"Well let me ask you, sir," I said real respectful-like, "suppose there had been a little tiny crack in that bowl for a long time and it kept getting bigger and bigger just waitin' to burst right open, and along comes Jack Moynahan, been unlucky all his life, and just happens to push that handle down for the last time before she blew, sort of like the millionth shopper at the A&P supermarket but instead of getting a prize he gets charged with destroying government property. It could have happened that way couldn't it, Mr. Parker?" I demanded.

"'Tain't likely," he replied with a sneer.

And then I thought I had him. I stood right in front of him, looked right into his eyes and said, "Mr. Parker we're not dealing with likely in this case, we're talking about *beyond a reasonable doubt.* You understand that, don't you?"

Out of the corner of my eye I saw a couple of jurors smile and I felt real pleased with myself.

Mr. Parker sat back in his chair and said, "Son, I've known Jack Moynahan for twenty years, and I'd stake my life on the fact that he done it. There ain't a whisper of a doubt in my mind."

I looked back at the jury and the smiles were gone. I tried to act as if his answer didn't bother me at all, but I knew I'd lost the round. "Now tell me, Mr. Parker," I said, "you agree, don't you, that Mr. Moynahan didn't have a sledge hammer or a crowbar or a hatchet in his cell with him? All he had was the shirt and pants he was wearing, without a belt because you took that away from him, isn't that true?"

"Them's the regulations," he replied.

"He had a mattress, a pack of cigarettes, some comic books and his boots with no laces."

"That's regulations too," he asserted.

"What is?" I demanded.

"No shoe laces so he cain't hang hisself," he said with a broad grin.

I paced a few times back and forth in front of the jury box to increase the drama of my next question, "Now will you please tell this jury, Mr. Parker, how you claim Mr. Moynahan broke that toilet bowl with his bare hands?"

"Never claimed he busted it with his bare hands. I figure he kicked it with his boot until he busted it."

I addressed the court, "Your Honor, may I have a brief adjournment to organize some evidence I would like to introduce at this time?"

"Seems as good a time as any to get up and stretch a bit, Counselor." He turned to the jury. "Now folks, we'll just give you a chance to get a cup of coffee in the jury room and have a smoke or whatever, so we'll stand adjourned for fifteen minutes."

I raced out to my car, opened the trunk and pulled out my exhibit, which I lugged back into the courtroom. I asked the clerk for an identification tag "Defendant's Exhibit A," and attached it to the exhibit. The judge had retired to his chambers for a few puffs on his favorite Havana cigar and maybe even a little pick-me-up from the Irish whiskey bottle he kept stored in the lower left-hand drawer of his desk. In due time he returned to the courtroom and instructed the clerk to bring the jury back in.

When they had settled down he turned to me and said, "All right, Mr. O'Leary, you may proceed with your cross-examination."

At that point I took the wrapping paper off the exhibit, which I had placed conspicuously on the counsel table.

"If the Court please, I offer in evidence Defense Exhibit A marked for identification," I said standing proudly beside a gleaming white toilet bowl.

Judge McDougal leaned forward, allowing his spectacles to slide down so he could see over the rims. Then he looked up at me and back down at the toilet bowl. "Now just what do you have in mind to do with that exhibit, Mr. O'Leary?" he asked in a not-too-friendly manner.

"Well sir," I replied, lifting the toilet bowl down and placing it in front of the witness stand. "I'm planning to ask Mr. Parker to step down here and show me how he claims the defendant kicked and busted the toilet."

"Approach the bench, Counselors," Judge McDougal said sharply.

When the prosecutor and I were huddled in front of the bench, the judge said, "Mr. O'Leary, I'll give you three minutes to get that abomination out of here. Jess Parker ain't on trial here. It's a cheap trick, and if you ever try to pull another stunt like that in my courtroom, I'll hold you in contempt and you'll get a chance yourself to try kicking one of them bowls in the county jail. Do I make myself clear, Mr. O'Leary?"

"Yes sir, but I thought . . ."

"I don't give a bejesus what you thought, young fella. You'll not be making a circus out of my courtroom, you hear me?"

"But . . ."

"There'll be no buts, Counselor. Now let's get on with it." The judge then turned to the jury and said, "Ladies and gentlemen, Mr. O'Leary has decided to withdraw his exhibit, and you may step down, Mr. Parker. Call your next witness, Mr. Hanrahan."

"I don't have any more witnesses, Judge. The People rest."

"That's your whole case, is it?" the judge asked.

Mr. Hanrahan nodded and said, "That's it, sir."

The judge then turned to me, "All right, Mr. O'Leary, call your first witness."

I was afraid if the jury learned that Mr. Moynahan had twenty-three prior D&D convictions they wouldn't believe a word he said so I decided not to put him on the stand. "The defense rests," I proclaimed.

"No witnesses, Mr. O'Leary?"

"No sir," I replied, perspiring.

"So be it," the Judge exclaimed. "All right, gentlemen, you may sum up. Mr. O'Leary first for the defense."

I explained to the jury that they were the sole judges of the facts, and that the district attorney's case was based entirely upon circumstantial evidence. I told them that Jack Moynahan was presumed to be innocent, that the prosecutor had the burden of proving that he did the dirty deed, and that they had to be satisfied beyond a reasonable doubt that it happened the way the prosecutor claimed before they could find my client guilty. When I sat down, the district attorney seemed to go on forever about law and order and how the jury should set an example by their verdict so our women and children could walk safely on our streets after dark. About an hour after the jury began to deliberate they sent word to the judge that they had a question. When they were seated again in the jury box the judge asked the foreman to rise and tell him what the jury wanted to know.

"Judge, we want to ask the defendant a question."

"I'm sorry, Lucas, but you can't do that. You have to decide this case on the evidence that's been presented."

"Well in that case, Judge, we've got a problem. The thing is we can't figure out how he done it."

The judge leaned back in his chair. Then he picked up the accusatory instrument, read it over carefully, took off his glasses and cleaned them with his handkerchief, put them back on and turned back to the jury. Lucas Haliday was still nervously standing in the box waiting for the judge to answer the jury's question.

"Well folks," he began, "I'm going to read to you exactly what this defendant is charged with, and I quote, 'The defendant Jack Moynahan is hereby charged with destroying government property on the 14th day of July 1979, in that he kicked and busted a toilet bowl in Cell 23 of the county jail.' Now, members of the jury, you have to decide whether or not the defendant did what they say he did. Does that clear things up for you?" the judge asked amiably.

The foreman looked around at his fellow jurors, who continued to look perplexed. The foreman shrugged his shoulders and replied, "I don't know, Judge. Maybe so." And the jury marched back into the jury room.

Twenty minutes later they sent word that they had reached a verdict.

"I understand from the court clerk that you have reached a verdict. Is that true, Lucas?" Judge McDougal demanded.

The foreman stood up, "Yes sir, we have," he replied solemnly.

"What is your verdict?"

"Well Judge, we all agree one hundred percent that the defendant done it, but we cain't figure out how he done it, so I guess our verdict is not guilty."

"Yeow," I whooped.

Judge McDougal rapped his gavel hard on the bench.

"That's enough, Mr. O'Leary," he admonished me.

"Sorry sir," I said, and quickly sat down beside my client. The judge dismissed the jury, and within five minutes the courtroom was deserted except for Mr. Moynahan and me. Since he had finished serving his sentence for being drunk and disorderly while he was awaiting trial, he was a free man. I just couldn't stop grinning. Finally we got up and walked over to the county jail to pick up the belongings that had been taken from Mr. Moynahan when they put him in his cell. The deputy emptied the contents of the big manila envelope on the counter. There was a worn leather belt, a bedraggled empty wallet, a broken ball point pen and $2.37. As soon as he signed for his meager possessions and we stepped outside the sheriff's office, Mr. Moynahan said, "Sure and it's time to celebrate, me boy. I'll stand ye to a brew at O'Malley's."

"Oh I'm afraid I can't do that, Mr. Moynahan. It's only two o'clock in the afternoon."

"Ah but I've got a killin' thirst after three weeks in the pokey, and besides I'm buyin', so ye can't refuse."

"In that case . . ." I shrugged, knowing we wouldn't be drinking for long on $2.37.

I expected the bar to be empty at that hour of the day, but there were a half dozen or more of Mr. Moynahan's cronies warming up for the twilight game between the Los Angeles Dodgers and the San Francisco Giants on television.

When Mr. Moynahan announced our victory, a great cheer went up. He declared me to be the most brilliant and courageous young barrister in the state and introduced me to all his drinking buddies.

"If Jack Moynahan says yer the best, then by Jesus, yer the best!" the bartender exclaimed. I felt compelled to buy a round of drinks, which cost me my monthly entertainment allowance, but I figured it was worth it because by the looks of Mr. Moynahan's friends it was very likely they would all need an attorney sooner or later.

We were on our third beer when Mr. Moynahan suggested that he had something he wanted to discuss with me in private. We slipped into a booth in the back of the bar where he took a hefty swig of his beer, pushed his cap to the back of his head, and said in a conspiratorial whisper, "Would ye like to know how I busted the toilet, Michael?"

I was taking a swallow of beer just as he asked the question and I almost choked to death.

"Now, now, it's not that bad, Michael. I never lied to ye. See son, there's a big difference between bein' innocent and bein' not guilty. The jury was right on the money when they decided I wasn't guilty, but I wasn't innocent either."

I remained silent, stunned by his remarks.

"As ye know, I've had occasion to visit the county jail more than a few times during me life and I can tell ye that it is the most boring place in the world. You just sit on yer arse in yer cell all by yerself with nothin' to do 'cept look at yer miserable life and count the days until ye can get back out. It's solitary confinement, is what it is, without the black dungeon part of it. And ye try to think up ways to make the hours pass. So what do ye think I did?" he asked, grinning.

"You broke the toilet . . . and you swore to me, Mr. Moynahan, you swore to me on the blood of Jesus, Joseph and Mary that you never busted that toilet." I spit out the words to him with real anger rising up inside of me. "You lied to me, sir, and I'm ashamed that I deceived those six good people trying to do justice."

"Now ye just hold on to yer breeches, Mr. Big Attorney. I told ye I wouldn't lie to ye and I didn't, and if ye'll get down off yer high horse for a minute I'll teach ye something about the law. I was charged with bustin' the damn toilet by kicking it with me boot and by God I didn't do that. What I did was to take some of them comic books that I had read a hundred times over—some o' them had been there from the first time they locked me up forty years ago. So I sat there one marnin' longin' for a drink of ice cold beer and cursin' the system that put me in jail for having a little fun on a Sadiday night. Now if ye want to hear the rest of the story yer gonna have to stand me to another beer because I've spent all me hard-earned money celebratin' our victory."

I stepped up to the bar, put a dollar down, got two beers and forty cents in change. I eased back into the booth and slid the brew across the table.

"Thank you, lad," he said as he took a swallow of beer and settled back in the booth. "Now where was I . . . oh yes. . . . So I was sittin' there commiseratin' with meself and I got an idee how to get even with the peckers. As I say, I took a bunch of them old comic books, crumpled 'em up and tossed 'em in the toilet. Then I lit a cigarette and tossed the match onto them comic books floating in the toilet. When the fire got goin' real good and hot, I flushed the shitter and the cold water come rushing in against the hot bowl and CRACK she went . . . just like I figgered she would. So was I guilty of breaking the damn crapper with me boot as charged? Not a bit I say. Was I innocent? Hell no I wasn't. Was justice done? Ah my young friend, I must tell ye, that is a matter that has been preying on me mind right serious. So tell me how much would ye charge me to prepare me will?"

"My fee for a simple will is ten dollars, but—"

"I know . . . yer wondering why I need a will when I don't have a penny to me name . . . right?"

"I didn't mean—"

"Sure ye did and it's all right 'cause it's the truth, 'cept what ye don't know is that during the course of me too-long life I spent thirty years at sea. That's where they give me the name *Jack O' Hearts*. And do ye know how come they did that?" I shook my head no. "Cause I'm a one-eyed Jack and there's onliest two, one-eyed Jacks in a poker deck and one of 'em is the Jack O' Hearts. So that's why they called me *Jack O' Hearts*. Now listen up son. Ye see, I been living on me seaman's pension but I've also got a five thousand dollar paid-up life insurance policy and nobody to leave the money to. So here's me proposition. I want ye to make out me will and handle me affairs when the good Lord decides to call in me marker. When I'm gone, ye'll pay yerself five hundred dollars for the will and whatever legal business there is to be done. Then out of the forty-five hundred dollars what's left ye'll give the county whatever it costs to replace the toilet—with interest, mind ye. And then I want ye to take the rest of the money and set up the *Jack O' Hearts'* Memorial Prison Library Fund, so that the inmates will have somethin' more upliftin' to read than Blondie and Dick Tracy."

"You got yourself a deal, Mr. Moynahan," I said, shaking his hand.

"Oh, there is one last little thing I'll be askin' ye to do," Jack Moynahan said, taking a long swallow of beer and smiling at me innocently. "One of the books I want ye to buy for me library is *How to Win at Poker* by Harry Finnegan. Now, on the inside cover ye must inscribe these words: 'This book will teach ye that when ye play poker, only a full house or better can beat a flush, but on August 6, 1979, the Jack O' Hearts beat a flush.'"

"I'd consider it an honor, Mr. Moynahan," I replied, reaching over and shaking his wrinkled old hand. My lasting memory of that moment was the way the sun, shining through the window of O'Malley's bar, reflected off the two gold teeth of the *Jack O' Hearts*.

Chapter Three

DOC WAS ON CALL AT THE HOS-
pital over the weekend and then Michael had to go out of
town so they didn't get together again until their next chess
match.

Michael had the chessboard all set up and the drinks
ready to pour when Doc arrived.

"I've decided I don't much care for winter any more,
Mike," Doc said, stomping the snow off his boots in the
entrance hall.

"That's one view we share, anyway," Michael said,
helping Doc off with his heavy coat. Shortly after drinks
were poured, the chess games began. Michael lost two
games in a row.

"I guess I've had enough for one night," he shrugged.

"Your mind wasn't on the games or I couldn't have
won so easily. You're worried about whether or not I read
your short story, am I right?" Doc asked kindly.

"You read me like a book, friend."

"Relax, old man. I read it, and believe it or not I remember Jack Moynahan. He was a patient of mine. Tough old bird, but you couldn't help but like him. So whatever happened to him? Did you set up the library like he wanted?"

"Well, things didn't quite work out the way he had planned. You see—"

"Never mind, I don't think I want to know. But I guess I'm up to reading the next story."

"You mean it?" Michael beamed.

"Might as well, there's no such thing as being a little bit pregnant."

"I'm sure glad I let you beat me at chess tonight."

"You never *let* anyone beat you in anything, you big fraud," Doc said as he began to pull on the boots he had left to warm by the fire.

"By the way, did you ever know Smitty, the guy who ran the gas station across from Louie's Diner?"

"You mean Alton Westmuller Smith? Hell, yes, he serviced my car for years."

"The name of my story is *Smitty's*," Michael said, handing Doc a large manila envelope. "Almost every word in it is true."

"Almost every word is true, and it's written by a lawyer . . . incredible! Oh, I get it, you said 'almost.' Yeah, that's standard lawyer-talk."

Chapter Four

Smitty's

"It's the next place on the left," I said, as we came around the bend. The driver slowed down and stopped the car under the big oak by the side of the road that looked exactly as it had three years earlier. I got out, grabbed my duffel bag from the back seat and stuck my head in the passenger door window.

"Thank you, sir. I sure appreciated the lift."

"It was my pleasure, Corporal. Welcome home," the driver replied, as he waved and pulled back onto the highway.

I had made pretty good time considering I had left Camp Lejeune, North Carolina, less than twenty-four hours earlier. After a tour of combat duty in the South Pacific I was sent to Officer's Training School there. I was a month away from graduation when the bomb was dropped on Hiroshima and hostilities ended. The Marine Corps no longer had any use for additional officers and within a week I was headed home to Vermont as a civilian.

I glanced at my watch. I knew my mom would be in the kitchen preparing dinner and Pop would be coming home from work in another half hour. I threw my duffel bag containing all my worldly possessions over my shoulder and began to trudge along the rutted stone path up to the house. I was amazed at how everything looked just as I remembered it, because I had left home as an eighteen-year-old boy and was returning as a man. I smiled when I reached the house and saw Mom's geraniums in full bloom beside the front porch. I swear they are the biggest and brightest geraniums in the county. The smell of wood smoke assured me that she was still refusing to cook on an electric range, but I would have been disappointed if it had been otherwise.

I dropped my bag on the front porch and peered through the living room window. I knocked on the door and then stood aside so she wouldn't be able to tell who it was until she opened the door.

"Rick!" she screamed when she saw me. And then we were all wrapped up in each other's arms, and we were kissing and she smelled wonderful as always. It wasn't Chanel No. 5. It was better. Sort of a combination of freshly ironed linen and cinnamon and Ivory soap. When Pop arrived home our reunion wasn't as demonstrative, but the feeling of love was just as deep.

That night we had pork chops and homemade applesauce, baked potatoes with gobs of butter, peas from the garden, thick slices of home-grown tomatoes and onions and fresh-baked bread. We finished the meal off with Mom's special apple pie, which I had dreamed about for three years.

After a week of sleeping past bugle call every morning, spending my days wandering aimlessly around the mountain that began its ascent outside our back door, and a few evenings telling war stories at the local watering hole, I figured it was time to look for a job. One night while I was scanning the want ads in the local newspaper I spotted a public notice that the Town of Brattleboro was going to auction off one of its dump trucks. Price controls on all vehicles were about to be abolished, and since no new civilian trucks had been manufactured for four years I thought I might be able to make a sizable profit by buying the truck at controlled prices and selling it as soon as the market became free again.

On the day of the auction two of us bid up to the controlled price limit and we broke the tie by flipping a coin. I won the toss and became the proud owner of a faded red 1940 Chevrolet ten-ton dump truck with the words "Town of Brattleboro" emblazoned on its driver's side door. It had just under 100,000 miles on the odometer and it looked a little tired, but the engine sounded fine and except for some rust beginning to show up on the rocker panels, it was in pretty good shape. One thing for sure, Vermonters take care of their machinery, so I knew it had been well maintained during the war.

After a few days of looking at that old truck sitting in the driveway doing absolutely nothing, I decided to put it to work until price controls were rescinded. During the first two weeks I was only able to pick up a few odd jobs, but then I received a call from a contractor who hired me to haul gravel. I ran that old truck twelve hours a day, six days a week, and was piling up the dough beyond my wildest dreams. It looked liked the job was good for at least three months because they were building a new road just over the Vermont border in New York.

It was at the end of my third week on the job when it happened. I had been pushing the truck pretty hard since before sunup, and it was the last run of the day. Since payment was being made on a "per ton delivered" basis, the more gravel I could squeeze into that sucker the more money I made, so I filled her to the brim on every trip. I planned to dump my final load at the site and head back home in time to open a cold brew and watch the sun go down.

I usually took the long way around Snake Mountain, which was one of the highest peaks in the state, but I decided if I went up and over instead of skirting around it, I would cut almost ten miles off the trip. It was hot, dusty, slow going in low gear as I climbed the mountain. When I finally reached the summit, I took a short break to let the engine cool down. I pulled into a rest stop, jumped down out of the cab and lit up a cigarette. For a dime you could look through a telescope and see New York to the west, Massachusetts to the south and New Hampshire to the east. As I leaned my elbows on the railing that surrounded the observation deck, spellbound by the view in every direction, I wondered why anyone in his right mind would want to live in a big, dirty, crowded city.

I stubbed out my smoke, tore up the paper and tossed the remaining tobacco to the wind. Then I climbed back in the truck, feeling pretty good about the direction my life was taking.

I picked up speed as soon as I started down the winding mountain road. As I came upon the first sharp curve, I pumped the brakes gently, but there was no response. I jammed my foot on the brake pedal clear to the floorboard and pulled on the emergency brake as hard as I could. All my brakes were gone! I had been in a few tough spots overseas, but I can tell you that being at the wheel of that old Chevy truck hurtling down the mountainside with over twelve ton of number-two stone in my back seat scared the living shit out of me. The needle on the speedometer hit fifty and continued to climb. The engine screamed when I double-clutched and down-shifted into second gear, trying to reduce my speed in order to regain control. There was a rock wall on my right, a sheer drop of five hundred feet or more on my left and a station wagon a couple hundred feet ahead of me. Although there was a guard rail on the cliff side of the road, I knew my rig would plow right through it like a hot steak knife through butter. If I tried to down-shift again at the speed I was traveling I'd rip the teeth right off the gear wheels. I tried to hug the cliff wall, but every time I encountered another curve, centrifugal force drove me into the opposite lane. When I came out of the last curve, the station wagon was only sixty feet ahead of me. I was steering with my left hand and holding the stick shift in place with my right, because if it popped out of gear I knew I would never be able to engage it again. I leaned on the horn with my elbow, hoping the driver of the wagon would recognize my plight and speed up out of harm's way, but instead he slowed down. My only options were to ram the wagon in the rear or pass it on the blind curve and pray. I elected prayer and steered into the opposite lane. As I came abreast of the wagon I got my first glimpse of the road ahead. An old bus was lumbering up the mountain a couple hundred yards away. I slammed my foot down on the clutch pedal to disengage the engine, and the truck lurched forward with an extra burst of speed enabling me to maneuver back into my lane a few feet ahead of the station wagon. I was freewheeling over seventy miles an hour, but by the grace of all that is sacred I found myself heading into an uphill straightaway, and then a gentle downgrade into the center of the village of Glenwood Landing.

I was drenched in sweat when I pulled up in front of the first garage I came to.

A dilapidated sign above the double bay doors announced that the owner was Alton Westmuller Smith. The place was called Smitty's.

I had paid seven hundred dollars for the truck but I didn't have a clue as to how much it was going to cost to put it back on the road. After paying for my gas and all, I had been clearing about twenty-five dollars a day. It was twice as much as my old man was making, but of course I was spending it all, because the war was over and I was alive and what the hell.

I went into the tiny office in the garage and asked to borrow the phone. "Smitty" nodded his approval and I called the construction foreman and told him what had happened. He cursed me out because he had kept a crew of men an extra hour waiting for the gravel. I told him I was sorry and I would try to make it up to him somehow, but he just hung up on me. I figured that at the ripe old age of twenty-one I was staring bankruptcy right in the eye.

Smitty had overheard the conversation,

stopped what he was doing, slowly wiped the grease off his hands, took a long swig out of an open quart bottle of Budweiser beer sitting on his workbench, belched loudly and said, "That yours?" nodding his head in the direction of my ailing truck.

"Until the bank takes it away," I replied.

"Kinda young to be owning a truck like that, aren't ya son?"

"Yeah, I got three hundred dollars mustering out pay in it. My old man co-signed the note for the balance," I said glumly.

"Well," he said taking another swig of beer, "you stopped at the right place. We can fix her up good as new."

I leaned against the desk that was cluttered with empty beer bottles, full ashtrays and various invoices scattered around in disarray.

"I'm sure you can," I said, "but the problem is that when you finish the job I assume you want to get paid."

"You're right about that . . . no tickee no shirtee," he replied smiling.

"That's the problem, I ain't got no tickee."

He finished off the bottle of beer and belched contentedly again. He hitched up his grease-stained pants, which were hanging precariously below a well-earned beer belly. "How about we go see how bad the situation is," he said, putting a gentle hand on my shoulder. We walked together over to the truck which still looked okay from the outside, but I knew how sick she was inside.

I lifted the hood and then climbed up into the cab.

"Start her up," he said. After only a few seconds he signaled to turn the engine off. I hopped down out of the cab and anxiously awaited his verdict.

"She's blown a head gasket," he said taking off his Pennzoil cap. He ran his fingers through his few strands of grey hair and replaced his cap, pulling the brim down over his forehead. Then he leaned over and spit out some tobacco juice, hitched up his pants with his elbows, and scratched his rear end.

"Needs new rings for sure," he said. "The pistons are probably scored—gotta take down the engine to tell that. At the best you are looking at a couple hundred bucks. At the worst, with the transmission and brakes, I don't know, four maybe five hundred," he said shrugging his shoulders.

"Jesus H Christ," I exclaimed.

"You got that right, son," he said sympathetically.

I crossed my arms over my chest and leaned against the front fender. "How would you like to buy a truck and a load of gravel. . . . I'm selling cheap." I wasn't joking.

He spit again and said, "Come on in the office. Let's see what we can figure out here."

As we ambled back into the office I wondered how he could drink beer and chew tobacco at the same time.

He sat down behind his desk in a rickety old high-back chair with stuffing erupting out of the cushion. "Sit down," he said, indicating an upended oil crate beside his desk. He pulled a spiral notebook out of one of the desk drawers, sharpened a pencil with his pen knife and blew on the end of the pencil. He opened a catalog on his desk and began to write in his notebook.

I studied the tiny office while he worked on his figures. A 1942 Petty Girl calendar was hanging on one wall and a 1944 Varga Girl calendar on the other. There was a gumball machine, an empty parrot cage and a large old refrigerator which I later learned was continually stocked full with Budweiser beer. Smitty threw down his pencil and demanded, "How much money have you got?"

"You mean on me or to my name?" I chuckled.

"What I am asking is how much have you got that you can put into fixing up this old crate of yours?"

"I got ten dollars in my pocket and sixty, maybe seventy bucks in the bank. That's the whole shootin' match."

He went back to his calculations, erased a few numbers and leaned back in his chair. I waited anxiously, knowing that this old grease monkey had me by the whatevers.

"The way I figure it, if you can come up with $82.18 we can probably solve this here problem," he said solemnly: "$72.18 gets you the parts and I'm gonna charge you ten dollars for the use of my tools and me telling you what to do and you're gonna do everything else yourself. It shouldn't take you more than a week or so."

"You mean it . . . oh, man . . . " I couldn't believe my good luck.

"So, have you got a place to stay?" he asked. Before I had a chance to answer, he added, "I got a bunk in the loft up above the shop. Some nights when I work late and have a few extra beers I sleep up there. You are welcome to it if you want. Of course I wouldn't object if you swept up in the morning, you know, kinda tidied up the place before we open."

"You got it," I said, smiling big, and we shook on it.

By the end of the first day I discovered that Smitty was a colossal drunk. He started to drink beer at eight o'clock in the morning when he opened the station, and never quit drinking until he closed up shop and went to bed at night. How he managed to consume gallons of beer day after day with no ill effects was beyond me. One thing was for certain, he was a first-class mechanic, and he taught me how to tear that engine down and put it back together so it ran like a Swiss watch. During that week he would often call me over on the pretense of needing me to help him with one job or another, but I knew that he really didn't need me; it was just his way of teaching me how to diagnose an engine problem, adjust a carburetor or install a new brake shoe.

When it came time to settle up my account with him he claimed that what I had done to help him on some of his jobs was about equal to what I owed him and our account was square. We both knew that it wasn't true, but I accepted his generous gift with a lump in my throat. He put his arm around my shoulder as we walked over to my truck. I started up the engine and we both listened to it purr for a minute or so before I looked down from the cab at that ugly old man who just stood there smiling up at me.

"See ya," I said, shifting into gear and moving out before he could see the tear I felt rolling down my cheek. When I checked the rear view mirror as I pulled out of the driveway, I saw him take off his old Pennzoil cap and sort of wave at me when he didn't think I could see him.

For several years whenever I could, I would fill up with gas at his station and we would jaw a bit together. Then I moved away and we lost touch, but I thought of him often. Later after my folks were gone and I was married with a boy of my own, I went back to Vermont to visit the old homestead and to see Smitty. I had told my nine-year-old son all about him and I wanted them to meet.

When we pulled into the village and drove over to the garage, it was all boarded up. I went across the street to Louie's diner where I had eaten every meal during that long-ago week, to see if I could find out where he was, and learned that during the previous winter he had suffered a heart attack pulling a transmission on a 1959 Mack ten-wheeler. He died right there under that truck with transmission fluid leaking down onto his cap and an open bottle of Budweiser just beyond his finger tips.

My son John and I walked back over to the garage and looked around. I told him the story of how I blew the engine roaring down Snake Mountain and how Smitty had taught me how to put it back together. I pointed out the spot where I had worked on my dump truck and the loft where I had slept and then Johnny yelled, "Hey Dad, look what I found." He held up an old oil-stained Pennzoil cap. I took it from him, sort of wiped it on my jeans and stuffed it in my pocket. As we were leaving the gas station I swear I heard Smitty say, "You got to teach that boy of yours how to tear down an engine, you hear?"

"You got that right ole buddy," I whispered. I put my arm around my son's shoulder and we walked back to where our car was parked in front of the diner.

Chapter Five

IT SNOWED IN GLENWOOD ALL week. Schools were closed. There was a power outage for twelve hours and only the main roads were plowed. Late on Monday afternoon Michael called Doc.

"Doc. Don't try to struggle out to my place tomorrow night for our chess match because I'm sure they won't have my road open by that time. I've been parking my car out on the highway and hiking through the drifts up to my house. You know it's almost a half mile up to my place from the main road."

"It's good for your soul, and if you don't overdo it, it's good for your heart as well."

"My soul is unsalvageable, and I can't believe that trudging through four-foot drifts at ten degrees above zero can be good for anything. Be that as it may, I thought I'd grab a bite in town after work and then drop over to your place, if that's okay with Beth."

"How about coming over for dinner?"

"If you want to know the truth, I haven't done anything but shovel snow and eat Birds Eye dinners for the past three days. I would really enjoy some home cookin'," Michael said, hesitated, and then added, "Have you had a chance to read *Smitty's* yet?" He held his breath, waiting for Doc's answer.

"Honestly Mike, I haven't. It's been a hell of a week. I've been working eighteen hours a day since I last saw you. But if you promise to come to dinner and bring the wine, I guarantee I'll read your story before you get here. I've got it sitting right next to the john and I'll give it my full attention tomorrow morning."

"It's not the environment I would have chosen, but beggars are beggars. See you tomorrow night."

Although Michael left his office in what he thought would be plenty of time, it took him a half hour to travel the six miles to Doc and Beth's house. And it continued to snow. Beth opened the door as soon as he knocked.

"We had about given up on you," she said after he snaked out of his snow-covered coat and kicked off his boots. She kissed him on the cheek and led him by the hand over to a roaring fire.

"God, everything smells so good."

"Am I included in that?" Beth asked, wafting a limp wrist past his nose.

"You are now," he laughed. "Where's the old man?"

"Fixing the drinks. As soon as he heard you clumping up the porch steps he ran to the bar. He's been threatening to start drinking without you for the past half hour." Michael smiled as Doc showed up with a tray full of drinks and a platter of crackers with warm Brie. The three of them settled in around the fire and held their glasses on high. "Cheers," they said in unison.

"I can't tell you how pleasant this is after a week of solitude, stuck up there in my mountain lair," Michael said, dipping a couple of crackers in the melted Brie.

"Mike darling, what you need is a good woman," Beth reached over and laid her hand over his.

"Is that an invitation?" Michael replied, giving her hand a squeeze.

"I hope so," Doc said. "Just think, if you took her off my hands I could start all over again with some sweet young thing that adores me and obeys my every command and waits breathlessly for me to return home each evening, standing by the door in her negligee with my favorite drink in her hand and a come-hither gleam in her eye. Oh Lord Mike, take her away."

"You know you couldn't get along without her," Michael responded.

"Just give me the chance," Doc said, opening his arms and rolling his eyes heavenward.

"I can tell you one thing, Lover," Beth quipped, "if

your chippy was waiting for you tonight in her negligee by the front door, she'd freeze her ass off." Even Doc couldn't keep a straight face.

"Seriously, Mike, it's time you know."

"I'll tell you the truth, Beth, I like the *idea* of marriage, it's the *reality* of it that scares me."

"Right on," Doc chimed in. "He'd rather show up at our monthly dine-around parties with a different gorgeous lady every time. Let's face it, Beth, he's got a tough life. But I like your plan to make him as miserable as the rest of us married guys. It is truly not fair to have him running around town with that silly-assed grin of contentment on his face. 'Oh Doc, I'd like you to meet Karen, she's a model in New York, you know—' 'Margie, come over here and meet my best friend Doc. Margie teaches sex therapy at the University, Doc. I'm taking private lessons you know. Ha, ha. What do you say Doc, is she lovely or not—' 'Doc, this is Louise, she dances the lead with the local ballet group—' 'Hey Doc, I want to show you something—'"

"That reminds me, Mike," Beth interrupted. "Marcia wants to know if you are bringing a date to her Christmas party."

"As a matter of fact I am coming all by myself, thank you. That way I'll be able to flirt with you and all the other married ladies."

They had another round of drinks, and by the time dinner was served, everything was overcooked but nobody cared. When they returned to the fire with cognacs all around, Beth said, "I've read your stories, Mike. They may not be Hemingway, but Doc says you have some more, and I think I'm ready for the next one. What is it called?"

"*Willow Run.*"

"Is it also about people from around here?"

"As a matter of fact it starts at a party we all went to at Katie Wycoff's house. Do you remember? She wanted us to meet her British actress friend."

"You mean the woman who kept her dark glasses on all through dinner?" Beth asked.

"That's the one."

"Hey, I remember her. She was gorgeous," Doc said.

"Oh, of course Casanova here wouldn't forget her," Beth said, shaking her head.

"You guys sure had me fooled, I thought you were the perfect couple."

"We are," they said in unison.

Michael lived outside the village in a farmhouse that was built before the Civil War. It sat on a knoll high enough so that he could see the spire of the Presbyterian Church in the center of the village. He owned close to two hundred acres of land, only a small part of which was cleared for growing hay and vegetable crops. There wasn't a level floor or plumb wall in the home, but Michael cherished every square inch of it.

He and his young wife Hannah had restored it to its

original condition, which meant scraping away layers of wallpaper that had accumulated over the years, tearing up the linoleum in the huge kitchen and bathroom, and then sanding and varnishing the wide pine boards that had been covered over a generation before. They went to auctions almost every weekend and bought bits and pieces of furniture that had managed to survive a hundred years and just needed to be refinished. One of their prize acquisitions was a hand pump Michael connected up to the kitchen sink for the children.

As he began to dress for the Christmas party he glanced at Hannah's picture on his dresser and was reminded that it was just before Christmas that he had lost her, a victim of a drunk driver on an icy road.

His marriage to her had been the best. Although the sharp pain of Hannah's loss was gone, the emptiness remained. He wasn't fixated on the memory of her, but he had given up hope of finding someone who could match her gentleness and spirit. At age forty-six, with both children gone from the nest, he was comfortable with his lifestyle. However, there were times when he longed for a woman with whom he could share more than his bedroom. "Like someone to help me with the laundry and the grocery shopping," he laughed to himself.

A light snow began to fall as Michael left home for Marcia's party. When he walked up the steps to her verandah and entered the crowded living room, the affair was in full swing.

The temperature outside had dropped to three degrees above zero, but there was a fire blazing in the hearth and the room smelled of apples and balsam. Doc was already at the piano leading a robust chorus of "Deck the Halls."

Michael headed for the kitchen where he knew the bar would be, poured himself a healthy Stolichnaya on the rocks and dropped in three onions. When he returned to the living room he took pleasure in greeting the guests as if he hadn't seen them in years, when in fact it was impossible to live in Glenwood without running into each of them regularly at the grocery store, the post office, Louie's Diner or the local watering hole, appropriately called The Dipper. These were all his friends. He had grown up with many of them, who had chosen to remain in the small village because of the quality of life which the presence of the university brought to the community.

He smiled as he glanced around the room, then he ambled over to the piano and joined in a rendition of "Rudolph the Red-Nosed Reindeer." Doc nodded appreciatively when Michael added his deep baritone to the chorus of voices. As they began to struggle through "O Holy Night," he noticed a woman he didn't recognize, chatting casually with Ben Wharton, president of Glenwood's major bank. At that moment she turned and looked directly at him from across the room. He raised his glass to her but she did not respond and quickly turned back to renew her conversation with Ben. "Snooty city slicker probably," Michael muttered, embarrassed by the rebuff. He continued with the group of songsters and after they finished "The Twelfth Day of Christmas," he headed back to the bar for a refill. When he entered the kitchen the woman was there, struggling to open a bottle of white wine.

"Here, let me do that," Michael offered. She handed him the bottle and the corkscrew.

"Thank you," she said, as he deftly removed the cork, held it briefly to his nose and poured a glass of wine. As he handed it to her he said, "I'm Michael O'Leary." Recognizing her striking resemblance to Ben's wife Martha, he added, "You must be Martha Wharton's younger sister."

"You are right about the family but flatteringly wrong about the relationship. Actually it was I who changed Martha's diapers, as they say. In fact, there is another sister even younger, but I shouldn't be giving away family secrets so quickly," she said smiling. "I'm Lucette Graham. It's nice to meet you. Thank you for coming to my rescue. Somehow or other I always manage to break up the cork into little pieces which float around in my glass until the bottle is empty."

"Yes, well, I've done that a few times myself."

"Will you join me in a glass of wine?" she asked, picking up the bottle and starting to pour out a glass for him. He quickly reached out to stay her hand, "No thank you. I am addicted to vodka, which does wonderful things for my personality while it muddles my brain and destroys my liver."

She was a tall woman, around thirty-five years old, he guessed, but the crinkles around her eyes seemed incompatible with the trimness of her body. She had chestnut-colored hair with what appeared to be natural copper highlights, but of course only her hairdresser could tell for certain, Michael thought. Her lips were full, painted bright red and opened slightly in a smile as he continued to stare at her.

"Is something wrong?" she asked as she put the wine bottle back on the table.

"No, no . . ." Michael stammered. "I just realized how badly mistaken I was about you when I first saw you."

"Whatever does that mean?" she asked, frowning.

Michael filled his glass with ice cubes and a generous portion of vodka. "The truth is," he said, raising his glass to her, "that when I first saw you, you were talking with Ben and you looked in my direction. I smiled my most engaging smile at you which you totally ignored."

"Oh my goodness, I'm so sorry. You see, I'm blind as a bat. I may have been looking at you as Ben filled me in on the guests, but in my little world, if you are more than ten feet away from me you don't exist. If I've got it straight I think Ben said you are an attorney, a trial lawyer, am I right?"

"I'm not going to admit anything until I find out what you think about lawyers. In some people's view attorneys are classified somewhere between used car salesmen and camel drivers in the scheme of things."

"My former husband is a Wall Street lawyer so I suppose I have to admit I have mixed feelings."

"I hope you won't be offended if I say that the difference between what a Wall Street lawyer does and what I do is like the difference between Madonna and the Madonna Della Pieta."

"Perhaps I *am* a bit offended, because I know many very bright and honorable Wall Street lawyers and include some of them and their wives among my close friends. On the other hand I really don't know you or what you do, so I'm in no position to make a judgment." He felt the blood rush to his face. She was looking him straight in the eye and smiling devilishly. "Could we start this conversation over after I apologize to all the Wall Street lawyers, used car salesmen *and* camel drivers of the world?" he asked.

She laughed openly and held out her hand. "Perhaps there is a chance we can become friends despite your predilection to generalize," she said graciously.

Michael took her hand and led her over to the piano. Doc and the group had exhausted their repertoire of Christmas carols and had started down the list of Irish ballads. Lucette enthusiastically added a strong contralto voice to the chorus of "My Wild Irish Rose" which everyone around the piano applauded.

At the end of the evening Michael offered to take her home but she declined. "However, I would love to get all bundled up and tramp through the woods some time, if you like," she offered brightly.

"You're on. How long are you going to be in town?"

"Two more weeks. I leave right after the first of the year."

"Great. I'll give you a call next week and we can hike up Hogback Mountain. You'll meet my friend, Marc Cutler, the fire warden."

"Sounds wonderful," she said as if she meant it. "I'll look forward to your call."

It had stopped snowing some time during the night, but four inches of fresh snow had accumulated on the roof of the bird feeder outside Michael's bedroom window by morning. It was a stupendous day with a crystal clear, cloudless blue sky. The sun was strong, casting sharp shadows in its path. A small herd of deer stood motionless at the edge of the clearing. The only movement was a wisp of smoke that crawled up through the trees from his neighbor's barn a half mile away. "I hope Phil is in the smokehouse making my Christmas present," Michael said aloud as he gazed out his bedroom window. The thought of Phil Dunham's smoked ham reminded Michael that he was starved. He pulled on a clean pair of jeans, turtleneck sweater and denim jacket and ambled down to his big kitchen. He threw a half dozen slices of bacon in the pan, scrambled up some eggs and put two slices of bread in the toaster. The deer had boldly begun to forage in the garden not more than fifty feet from his kitchen window. He dished the bacon and eggs onto a big platter, buttered the toast and sat down to enjoy the food and watch the deer.

When he finished breakfast, he drove into town to pick up *The Sunday New York Times*. Upon his return there was a message on his answering machine from Beth inviting him over late in the afternoon for eggnog and some left-over turkey she had purloined from Marcia's party. "Don't forget to bring your story," she added at the end of the message. After settling in his favorite chair with the newspaper, he turned on television to watch the Redskins and the Bills. When the game was over, he stuffed all of his stories and a bottle of white wine into his briefcase and headed over to Doc's house.

After he handed Doc the wine and the envelope with *Willow Run* printed in bold letters on the outside, Beth dragged him into the kitchen to shell peas and peel potatoes while Doc read his story.

Chapter Six

Willow Run

I was seated beside an attractive woman at an elegant dinner party hosted by Katie Wycoff, the wife of the chairman of the Romance Languages Department at the university. Katie had informed me that one of my dinner companions was Sylvia Kent, a supposedly well-known British actress, though I had never heard of her. I judged her to be in her late thirties, but it is difficult to be certain about women of the theater wearing dark glasses. The gentleman on the other side taught in the Drama Department, and after brief introductions he and Miss Kent began to exchange gossip about stage and screen luminaries who were mutual friends of theirs. Left to my own devices, I allowed my mind to wander to the time I met "my" Sylvia. I remembered that I had been sulking, mean and unforgiving because my parents had demanded that I join them on their vacation in Vermont. My mother had arranged the holiday with an old college roommate who had invited us to their summer cabin. When I learned that I would be spending two weeks in the middle of the Green Mountains with nothing to do and no one to do it with, I had begged my parents to allow me to remain at home on Long Island, where I was a valued member of the Sea Cliff Seagulls, a nondescript collection of athletes who competed with the Roslyn Rascals and the Port Washington Pumas. I was almost sixteen years old and quite capable of taking care of myself, I argued. But my pleas fell upon deaf ears.

Shortly after our arrival at the cabin I stood in the shadows beside a mountain stream, mesmerized by the sight of the most beautiful creature I had ever seen in my short and sheltered life. She was arcing out over the churning water on a great rope swing tied to the branch of a gnarled old willow tree. She was slender, with radiant eyes, budding breasts and sleek limbs burnished by the summer sun. I watched silently as she pushed out over the creek again and again with amazing strength and grace. When she finally noticed me, she waved, jumped off at the base of the tree and scrambled up the bank beside me.

"Hi, I'm Sylvia. You're Jason . . . right?" she said with smiling emerald eyes.

"They call me Jake. I like that better."

"Okay, Jake. In that case you can call me Syl. . . . .Deal?"

"Deal!" I replied, returning her grin with one of my own.

In the days that followed she and I hiked to the top of Razorback Mountain, batted fly balls and grounders to each other in the meadow (she had her own glove), argued about the Brooklyn Dodgers (my team) and the New York Yankees (her team), rescued an injured baby raccoon, and spent three days damming up the creek they called Willow Run so we could have a swimming hole beside the ancient willow.

Every evening just before sundown we rounded up Mr. Tillotson's thirty-head of milking cows from the pasture just below our cabin, and drove them down to his barn. It was a big old rambling building that had been painted red once upon a time. Over the years it had turned silver, except at sunset when it shimmered like gold.

Syl and I usually did the dishes after dinner while the folks had their coffee, and then we all played hearts or Monopoly or charades. I had never known how much fun my folks could be.

Even my dad, who was usually pretty somber, seemed really laid back.

Each morning before breakfast Syl and I walked down to the farm for fresh milk. By the time we got there our sneakers would be soaked by the heavy morning dew that lay like silver lace over the pasture and the meadow. There were three big old pigs that mucked around in a pen under the barn and several dozen chickens that wandered free in the yard. We usually stopped in to see Mrs. Tillotson, who cooked on a massive wood stove that always had a pot of something going on it. The kitchen smelled of fresh-baked bread and laundered linen and strong coffee. There was a blue and white checkered oil-cloth on the big round table in the center of the kitchen where the family and the hired hand gathered for meals.

One morning we arrived before the milking was finished and Mr. Tillotson taught us both how it was done. First you sat down on a little three-legged wooden stool alongside and sort of underneath the cow, and pressed the side of your face up against her belly so that she couldn't blind you with her swishing tail. Next you squeezed the milk pail between your knees and grasped two teats, one in each hand, holding them just so between your thumb and your first two fingers. Then you eased them down until you saw the spurt of milk and heard the "plink" and "plunk" in the bottom of the pail. Syl got the hang of it faster than I did, which was very disconcerting since I was a boy and older and all. When I finally got both teats going in rhythm like Mr. Tillotson showed me, the damned cow kicked over the pail and the milk spilled all over the floor. I can still feel the heat of my failure, but I vividly remember the thrill of holding those fat fingers of soft warm flesh in my hands, and I've often wondered how the cows felt when they were switched over to the cold steel milking machines.

When the pails of milk were filled we poured them into ten-gallon cans and carried them into the milk room, where they were stored and cooled by fresh running water siphoned from the nearby creek.

One day we helped with the haying. It was a scorching hot summer day with the threat of rain in the evening, so the hay that had been cut had to be harvested before nightfall. For the first hour or so, pitching the hay up on the wagon was an exciting new adventure, but as the wagon filled, it became more and more difficult to heave the hay up on top of the load, and the pitchfork became heavier and heavier. I was a bit envious of Syl who got to drive the team of draft horses, though Mr. Tillotson told me confidentially that old Tim and Tom really didn't need much driving since they knew what to do on their own. Nevertheless she looked mighty important riding high on that wagon holding the heavy reins and calling out "gee" when they were supposed to turn right and "haw" when she wanted them to go left.

At noon Mrs. "T" brought us ham sandwiches and a big jug of cold lemonade. We gathered under an old chestnut tree in the center of the hayfield to eat lunch and Syl and I were feeling good about being part of it all. We had just started to relax after we finished eating but Mr. Tillotson and "Jumper," the hired hand, picked up their pitchforks and headed back out into the field, which didn't leave us any choice but to follow them. I guess they had their eye on me though, because just as I thought I wouldn't be able to lift another forkful of hay, Jumper sent me up on the wagon to distribute the hay as the men pitched it up. It was a much easier job, but even so, by the time we pulled the last load into the barn I was beat. I had certainly gained a deep and lasting appreciation of what it took to be a Vermont farmer in those days.

There was a shower at the cabin, made out of an oil drum which sat on top of four log posts. You hand-pumped water from the creek into the drum, took a deep breath and pulled on a rope to release the water. The pure joy of that rush of ice cold water washing away the prickly chaff on my weary sunburned shoulders sits up there near the top of my list of good things to remember in life. During dinner Syl and I could barely keep our eyes open and as soon as we finished washing the dishes we both went straight to bed.

On the day before we were scheduled to leave, we all squeezed into our old Buick and drove over to Somerset to see the Windham County Fair. It was a glorious day and people had come from all over the county to have their baked goods, fruits, vegetables and livestock judged. They came to compete in the wood-chopping contest and the horse-pull, and just to have a good time.

Bands from all the high schools in the county played continuously throughout the day, and there was a hilarious donkey race where the riders had to sit backwards on the donkeys. Two volunteer fire departments engaged in a water fight and then had a tug of war where the losers got dragged through the mud hole they had created.

There was a midway where Syl fell in love with the biggest teddy bear I had ever seen. I spent almost all of my money trying to win it for her, but all I got was a small stuffed dog which she immediately named Jake and swore to treasure forever.

We walked hand in hand through each exhibit, made our selection of the best calf, the cockiest rooster, and the fattest pig. We ate cotton candy, giant hot dogs, and buttered corn on the cob sold by the Ladies Aid Society of the First Presbyterian Church. We had our weight guessed, rode the Ferris wheel, and braved the dangers of the "Spook House."

Syl dared me to go into the tent to see the "Bevy of Naked Ladies." Although you were supposed to be over eighteen years old to be admitted, the ticket taker didn't hesitate to accept my quarter as I slinked in alongside two burly young farm boys. My heart was pounding in anticipation of what I was about to see. I had never seen a single live naked woman, let alone a "bevy" of them. "Sex education" wasn't invented until long after I didn't need it, and at that time my knowledge of the female anatomy was limited to what I had learned from a set of French postcards that had been circulated around the locker room in high school. I had a pretty good idea of the concept of sex; it was the mechanics of it that remained a mystery, you know, exactly where important things were located and all.

It was quite dark as we passed through the narrow entranceway which led to the "inner sanctum," as they called it. Once inside we were confronted with a canvas wall about eight feet high extending from one side of the tent to the other. There were eight large openings, each about the size of a watermelon, located at eye level along the wall. Two men with their backs to us already had their heads stuck through the openings. My mouth was dry and I could feel my heart pounding unreasonably fast as the three of us stepped up to look through the holes. I was about to see my first nude woman.

When I put my head through the opening I was shocked to find myself staring at a large mirror about ten feet away from me. The mirror reflected the inside of my viewing wall and I saw eight very well-endowed naked ladies, painted on my wall. Three of them were headless, and atop the voluptuous bodies of the other five were the faces of the five fools who were peering at them in the mirror. The lady directly opposite me, my twin sister, had an expression on her face that went quickly from disappointment to anger, until I saw my fellow voyeurs grinning and making idiotic faces at each other in the mirror. Finally "my" lady burst out laughing in chorus with her companions. What a bevy of beauties we were, and what a lesson to be learned at such an early age. The success of that wonderful con-joke depended entirely upon each victim's unwilling-ness to reveal the fraud, hoping I suppose that others would fall into the trap so that he would not stand out alone as the village idiot.

As I emerged from the tent still grinning, Syl wanted me to describe what I had seen. I said, "When you've seen one you've seen them all," and refused to say another word about it. I think she concluded that it was either too good or too bad to talk about, and she was right on both counts.

At night the sparkling lights on the midway turned the meadow into a fairyland. Our parents proposed that we all go to a restaurant in town, but we prevailed upon them to let us stay at the fair and be picked up after dinner. Then we quickly lost ourselves in the crowd before they could change their minds.

We watched the beauty contest where the County Queen was selected, and then as the beer tents filled up and the crowd got noisier and livelier, the Orleans Mountaineers, consisting of three fiddles, a drum, two harmonicas, and a trumpet, began to play the best hoe-down music in the state. The eager square-dancers immediately took to the makeshift dance floor and the place began to jump. Although neither Syl nor I had ever danced to the foot-stompin' country rhythms before, we were pulled in to join the fun by an old codger. He had to be pushing ninety, but he was one of the best dancers in our group.

In short order we were hootin' and hollerin' with the best of them. One time we found ourselves marching east while everyone else was marching west and we ended up in the center of the circle. We didn't know what we were doing, but we did it with such enthusiasm that the group egged us on until our legs turned to jelly. Finally another couple took pity on us and replaced us in the circle and everyone gave us a big round of applause. We danced every dance, and then too soon, the Mountaineers played the last song, "Good Night Sweetheart." Syl and I danced cheek to cheek just like the older folks all around us. It was the first time I had touched Syl romantic-like, and it was something really special.

Unbeknown to us our parents had returned

after their dinner intending to pick us up and head home, but when they spotted us having the time of our lives they just settled down on the weathered plank bleachers with the other spectators and waited for us to give up, but of course we never did until the very end.

As we danced the last dance, we sang the chorus together.

Good night sweetheart, till we meet tomorrow.
Good night sweetheart, parting is such sorrow.
Tears and sadness may make you forlorn
But with the dawn, a new day is born
So I'll say Good night sweetheart . . . Good night.

As the music ended, Syl looked up at me and I bent down and kissed her forehead. She squeezed my hand tight and I led her off the dance floor, where our parents miraculously appeared. I didn't understand why our mothers were smiling, misty-eyed, and our fathers looked so grim.

There wasn't much talk on the way home. I sat between the men in the front seat and Syl fell asleep with her head on her mother's shoulder in the back as we twisted and turned through the hills of Vermont on that long ago night. We picked up the eyes of a coon or maybe a young fox in the headlights once and a herd of deer leaped across our path as we turned into the long dirt road leading up to the cabin.

Syl and I went off to bed while our parents said their farewells over coffee in the kitchen. Just as I was falling asleep, I heard a scratching noise and a note was slipped under my bedroom door. I took the note over to my bedside lamp and opened it.

> *Jake,*
> *Please meet me at the*
> *Swing Willow at 1:00.*
> *Syl*

I glanced at my watch. It was 11:35. Suddenly I was wide awake, my heart racing with the danger of the scheme. I know that it is difficult for you in these days to think that a strong boy who was almost sixteen would be frightened by the prospect of being caught sneaking out of the cabin, but I can tell you now that my delight at the prospect of the adventure was equaled by a blinding yellow fear that sent chills to all of my extremities.

My room was on the second floor of the cabin with a window looking over the front porch roof. It was a simple matter to get out on the roof; the problem was that I would have to crawl under Syl's parents' bedroom windows in order to reach the trellis where I could climb down to the ground.

I heard the adults coming up the stairs around midnight. By 12:15 the lights were all out and there was absolute silence throughout the house. At 12:45 I stepped out on the porch roof with the sound of my heart pounding in my ears. I held my breath, lowered my head and body below the window sill and crawled stealthily to the end of the porch roof without mishap. I climbed down the trellis and quickly jogged down the path to the willow tree. Syl was already there when I arrived.

"You're crazy," I whispered.

"You came," she said, grinning.

"That makes me crazy too," I said.

She leaned back against the crooked old willow, her arms at her side looking straight up at me with those oversized cat's eyes that picked up specks of moonlight like phosphorous dancing in a night sea.

We stood silently gazing at each other. I thought my heart would burst with love for her.

"I wanted you to kiss me goodbye properly," she whispered. And then she was in my arms. I could scarcely breathe, my legs were melting as she reached up and pulled my head down. I kissed her hard and then she opened her soft lips, inviting me to experience my first deliriously erotic grown-up kiss. I desperately wanted to caress the rosebuds that were pressed so tight against my chest, and I ached to explore the soft petals of her innocence . . . but I did not.

We held that single exploring kiss for an eternity, and then she whispered, "I love you," and slipped out of my arms and was gone into the night. "I love you, I love you, I love you . . ." I cried into the darkness and then I sat down on the roots of that old willow and tears slid down my cheeks because it was the most beautiful thing that had ever happened to me.

In the morning we all said our good-byes, promised to write and to make plans for the following summer. After returning home, we exchanged a few short letters before the summer holidays ended, but when school began, I guess we each got caught up in new adventures, and all that was left of our brief affair was a memory that I would savor whenever I heard the name Sylvia.

It's amazing, I thought, as I gazed around Katie's lavish dinner table, how my vision of that long ago summer adventure was so clear in my mind that I could still taste the sweetness of that kiss upon my lips.

When dessert and coffee were being served, Miss Kent turned to me.

"Now I think it is our turn to get to know one another, Dr. Donnelly," she said graciously.

"I'd like that," I replied.

"Katie tells me that you are a forensic psychiatrist but she neglected to tell me what forensic psychiatrists actually do. I don't even know where my forensic is," she said.

I smiled and replied, "I would be pleased to help you find it if you wish."

"Oh my, I think we best postpone that search until we're better acquainted, don't you?" she said, taking a sip of wine.

"Why don't we begin that process right now," I replied immediately. "For instance, is this your first visit to America?"

"Oh no, I have been here many times over the years but this trip has been my most unhappy visit. I'm here trying to settle the affairs of my late husband's estate. He was born in America, and although we lived in England, he had many business interests here."

"Do you miss England?" I asked, trying to keep the conversation going.

"I haven't been back home in almost a year and I miss it dreadfully," she replied sadly.

"So you are both British and American?"

"Quite right. Except for a few years while I was growing up, I have spent my whole life in England."

"As a matter of fact," I said, "I was just thinking about a young girl named Sylvia whom I met many years ago. The name Sylvia always creates sylvan images for me . . . Vermont . . . cool forests, white birch trees in the mist, wild horses with manes flying, racing across a meadow, falling autumn leaves, sparkling mountain brooks. . . ."

"My goodness, that sounds delightful. But are you certain that it's the name and not the girl you knew who creates those images for you?" she asked.

"No, it's the name all right. On the other hand, as I think about it, I'm sure you would be just as beautiful if your name were Hermione or Hepzekiah," I said.

"Now really, Dr. Donnelly, I'm flattered of course but . . . Hermione and Hepzekiah?"

"All right then . . . I know your stage name is Sylvia, but what is your real name?" I asked.

"Believe it or not . . ." she said, sliding her

dark glasses down and looking directly into my eyes, "my real name . . . is Sylvia." She laughed a deep husky laugh that sent tiny shock waves down to my fingertips. And then it struck me, those eyes she had kept hidden all evening, and that wonderful laugh. . . .

"Miss Kent . . ." I stammered.

"But now that we have gotten to know each other so intimately, you must call me Syl."

I held my breath as she reached over and picked up my place card, turning it between her fingers. "Jason Donnelly," she whispered thoughtfully.

"My friends call me . . ."

"Jake!" she gasped, reaching out and covering my trembling hand with her own.

A few days after our reunion at Katie's dinner party I had to testify in a murder case being tried in Texas. Sylvia and I had exchanged telephone numbers and I called her several times upon my return to New York, but was unable to reach her. After a few weeks of telephone tag, I finally wrote her a long letter describing exactly what a forensic psychiatrist does, but it was returned to me with the notation "addressee unknown." I decided she had probably returned to England, and I sadly pigeonholed the affair to be dealt with in my next life. However, a few months later I received a nice note from Katie with an enclosed letter marked "Personal."

Dear Jake,

I tried calling you before coming back to London but all I got was a darn machine telling me you were forensicing with some woman in Texas. Then in the confusion of moving I lost your telephone number and address and have asked Katie to forward this letter on to you. I know that Thomas Wolfe taught us that we can't go home again, but I just purchased a two-hundred-year-old cottage about eighteen kilometers north of Broadway in the Cotswolds and I'm thinking of building a rope swing over the stream that runs through my property. Are you available as a consulting engineer?

Fondly, Syl

I went into the kitchen, put a few ice cubes in a rocks glass and filled it to the brim with Boodles gin. I took my drink into the den, settled back in my favorite chair and reached for the telephone.

"British Airways, good evening, may I help you?"

"Yes ma'am, I'd like to make a reservation from New York to London."

"Your name please?"

" Jason Donnelly."

"When would you like to depart, Mr. Donnelly?"

"When is your next flight?" I asked.

"Flight 439 leaves Kennedy International Airport at 6 P.M. this evening," she answered brightly. I glanced at my watch. It was three minutes past four o'clock. "Put me on it," I said immediately.

"And when would you like to return, sir?" she inquired pleasantly.

"Well now, I'm not sure about that. You know, it all depends."

Chapter Seven

WHEN MICHAEL'S KITCHEN chores were completed he wandered back into the living room where Doc was still reading *Willow Run*. Doc ignored him until he finished the story. After he put it down on the coffee table, he sat staring into the fire.

"So what do you think?" Michael asked, hesitantly.

"This is what I was worried about all along, damn it. I don't believe you want to hear what I think."

"Of course I do," Michael lied.

"Okay, do you really think anyone under forty could read your story and believe that a sixteen-year-old boy who wasn't retarded could be as immature as your Jake was? Hell, these days they start in the seventh grade. I know because I'm treating eleven- and twelve-year-old kids for chlamydia infections, and, God help me, I have a fifteen-year-old girl with genital herpes and a fourteen-year-old boy with gonorrhea."

"I realize that times have changed drastically, but I told it the way it was, the way it used to be. I think the old way was better, but who knows? So tell me, aside from the generation gap problem, what else?"

"Well, to be honest, the other thing is, I don't like to be left hanging at the end of the story. I mean, so how does it end?"

"That's the whole idea, the reader makes up his own ending. What do you want me to do? Should I have ended the story . . . 'and they lived happily ever after'?"

"Sure, why not? I like that."

"But suppose they didn't. Suppose that Jake got killed in an auto accident on his way from the airport to the lady's home. Or more likely, suppose after a couple of months of living together, when the testosterone settled down, they discovered they didn't have a damn thing in common except their memories. After all, Jake was a bachelor most of his life. I can tell you it isn't easy to change your ways after years of being a bachelor."

"You ought to know."

"That's the point. I do know, and as much as I would like to believe they fell madly in love all over again, let's face it, what the hell did they know about each other when he decided to fly over to England? They had spent a week together when she was fourteen or fifteen years old, then they didn't see each other for twenty years, they spent one hour reminiscing, and you expect them to fall in love again, get married and walk into the sunset holding hands, is that it?"

"Yeah, something like that. I'm a sucker for a happy ending," Doc laughed.

"Well, I can assure you that in real life people don't fall in love just like that. It takes time to get to know one another, it doesn't happen overnight. I mean you have to take into account things like religious and political beliefs, career objectives, personal habits like smoking and drinking. . . . Love at first sight is a delightful myth, so I think I'm going to leave it the way it is and you can believe whatever you want about how it really ends."

"I'm beginning to understand why you haven't remarried, Mike, but maybe you're right. I sure as hell don't want to find out that she just wanted someone to help her build the swing and when it was finished she sent him packing. Anyway, at least this story had a little sex in it, although it was about as mild as you can get."

"You want sex? I'll give you sex." Michael went out to the hall entrance and brought back his briefcase, fished out another story and offered it to Doc.

"Oh no, Michael, I'm not ready for another one just yet. I think our friendship barely survived this last story. Give it to Beth, she's much better at this kind of thing." Michael flushed and said, "I'm pretty sure she won't like this next story."

"Why, because it's got some sex in it? She'll love it."

Beth came into the room carrying celery and carrot sticks, and dip. "What will I love?" she demanded.

"Mike's got another story, and I'm not up to it right now. He says it's got some sex in it and I said you would probably love it. I mean you can't tell me you read Danielle Steele for the prose, Beth."

"We middle-aged married ladies cope . . . *vicariously* I think it's called." Doc started to respond, but Michael interrupted him.

"Don't touch it, Doc, just let it lie there and fizzle out like a Fourth of July sparkler. If you pick up on it too soon, you're going to get burned. Here, read this please, Beth," Michael said, handing her the envelope. "Your old man and I are going to go down and play some pool."

"Now you're talking my language," Doc said with enthusiasm.

"Dinner will be ready in half an hour," Beth looked at the title and added, "*Malaysian Cocktail*. What's that supposed to mean?"

"Read it and weep." Michael said, dragging Doc down to the game room.

"A buck a point. Get out your wallet, Counselor."

 *Chapter Eight*

Malaysian Cocktail

His eyes followed the secretary as she entered the room and handed the check to the bank's attorney, who dropped it casually on the polished mahogany conference table. He was too far away to read the words on the check, but he knew what they said. "Pay to the order of Peter Doyle the sum of Two Hundred Fifty Thousand Dollars ($250,000.00)."

Peter could feel his pulse quickening as he thought, "It's really going to happen. In a few minutes he's going to hand me that check and I am going to walk out of this room with two hundred fifty thousand dollars in my pocket, and a promissory note which will pay me $37,500 a year for twenty years; that's $750,000. Does that make me a millionaire?" he asked himself.

"I'll need a check payable to the county

clerk for deed stamps, and . . ." Peter's lawyer Michael O'Leary prattled on, but Peter paid little attention as he filled out and signed the checks demanded of him.

"Here is the promissory note," his lawyer said, handing him the document.

"How much is that a month, Michael? I've lost track."

"Enough to spring for a few drinks at the club on Saturday," the bank's attorney replied.

"Sounds good to me," Peter said.

"Here it is, right here, $3,125 per month for twenty years," his lawyer said, and then whispered to Peter, "And the best part is that by putting it all in trust for your wife, Miriam, it becomes a totally tax-free transaction."

The bank's attorney slid the check down the table to Peter, who stared at it for a few moments, then picked it up and slipped it into his inside coat pocket. His lawyer gathered up the legal documents, they shook hands all around, wished each other well, and Peter walked out of the bank with enough money to retire.

But it wasn't a gift. It was the result of thirty-seven years of effort. Peter had begun his career in the retail shoe business as a stock boy after graduation from high school. He worked his way up in a few years to become the manager of a small store in Glenwood. After marrying Miriam Castleman, he fathered a child, and then borrowed enough money from Miriam's father to open his own shoe boutique. He called it "Georgio's." With a combination of skill, a sixty-hour work week and a bit of luck, he parlayed his one store into five shops. He sent his daughter to an Ivy League school and now he was cashing in his chips at age fifty-five. Shoe International, Inc., with 127 outlets in the U.S., had decided to purchase his small group of boutiques. It was the classic American success story.

After the deal closed, Peter and Miriam sold their mortgage-free home in Glenwood and bought a split-level with a faraway view of the Pacific in a gated community in Southern California near their daughter. With twenty years of guaranteed monthly income, and Social Security benefits to begin in a few years, they would be able to live out their early retirement lives in modest comfort. Peter was proud of his business achievements, but he considered the money in the bank a symbol of his success rather than the object of his life's efforts. "Money ain't everything," he often said.

Although they had been married for almost

thirty years, it was a successful marriage only with respect to its longevity. Miriam was lazy and self-indulgent. After the birth of their child she derived more pleasure in the kitchen than she did in the bedroom, and by the time she was thirty she had become considerably overweight. She claimed it was glandular and there was absolutely nothing she could do about it, but she never refused a second helping of anything, and spent a fortune on Fanny Farmer chocolates, Ben and Jerry ice cream and vodka martinis. She had never worked outside the home, and did as little work as possible inside it. When they moved to California, she spent her days shopping with their daughter, playing bridge, watching the soaps and gossiping at the hairdresser's. Peter filled his days with tending to his garden, building antique furniture reproductions in his wood-working shop and following his favorite team sports on television. And so this story should end with Peter and Miriam walking separately, but equally unhappy, into the California sunset. Actually, this is where the story begins.

Peter had just put a third coat of varnish on a reproduction of a sixteenth century armoire, and was sitting on his back deck with a tumbler filled with gin and ice watching the faraway Pacific Ocean swallow the sun.

"Peter!" Miriam called, as if she were hailing a taxi.

"I'm out on the deck," he answered, and watched Miriam waddle out and ease into the chaise lounge opposite him. "Somewhat like the Staten Island Ferry docking at the 69th Street Pier," Peter thought.

"You won't believe what I have done," she said as soon as she had caught her breath after the exertion of seating herself.

"Probably not. So tell me, what have you done?"

"I've hired a maid!" she replied.

"You what?"

"All our neighbors have Mexican women come in at least once a week, and I could use someone to help me with the grocery shopping, the cooking, the washing and ironing—"

"Hold it," Peter interrupted, "I don't give a rat's ass who works for our neighbors. And the facts are that I have been doing all the grocery shopping; we have pizza or Kentucky Fried Chicken at least three nights a week and the only iron you have had in your hand since we've been married is a five iron golf club twenty years ago."

"But that's the point, don't you see, Peter? Now with Maité's help. . ."

"Maité? Isn't that a tropical cocktail?"

"You mustn't make fun of her name, Peter. You spell it M-A-I-T-E with that little thing over the *e* which means you pronounce it My-tay. She is Malaysian, and she speaks French and English."

"Malaysian!" Peter exclaimed.

"Actually she was born and brought up in Thailand."

"What's she doing here?"

"Well, I was playing bridge with the girls yesterday, and Charlotte—"

"Charlotte?" Peter queried.

"You don't know her, but she's just darling. Anyway, Charlotte told us that her daughter lives in Malaysia with her husband who is Dutch for some reason or other, and when Charlotte went over to visit them everyone there was so friendly and the men were all handsome and everyone wears flowers in their hair, including the men, and Charlotte met this wonderful waitress at her hotel and she invited her to come to the States and work for her, and after doing all the paper work and getting Maité a visa and everything, and paying for her ticket to come to California, wouldn't you know the day after Maité arrived, Charlotte's husband, he works for Mobil Oil Company, you know—"

"No, I didn't know," Peter shrugged.

"Anyway, he does and he makes oodles of money, and Charlotte's son-in-law works for Shell Oil Company, isn't that interesting?"

"Fascinating."

"And Charlotte's husband—his first name is Monroe or Morgan or some such, and he just got word that he is being transferred to Abu Dhabi, that's somewhere in Egypt, you know."

"I don't think so," Peter sighed.

"Whatever; so there was poor Charlotte, and Maité just arrived with all her baggage and so happy to be in America the land of her dreams, and Charlotte was in tears as she was telling the story because she didn't know how in the world to tell poor Maité that she was going to have to turn around and go right back to where she came from. And that's when I said, 'I'll take her for one day,' and then all the girls chimed in and each took a day and Charlotte said how wonderful we all were, and that's the whole story."

"A regular fairy tale," Peter scoffed.

"That's what all the girls said, and I'm

picking her up at Charlotte's house tomorrow morning."

"Of course it's a minor matter, but where is Mata Hari planning to live?"

"Maité, her name is Maité, and I was just coming to that. I told them that you were such a wonderful woodworker and we have that space over the garage that's just going to waste, so I said we could take her and she could have her own little apartment. Everyone thought that was a fantastic idea and they're all going to contribute furniture and linens and all."

"What about the cost of the plumbing, heating and wiring?"

"It can't be all that much and Maité is going to work for us an extra three days a month to pay us like rent."

"And what happens if it turns out we don't like her?"

"We are going to love her and she is going to love us. Charlotte says so," Miriam said forcefully.

"Charlotte doesn't know me, which is probably a good thing for both of us," Peter said. "So how old is she and what does she look like?"

"I think she is in her early twenties, but I don't know what she looks like. However some of the most beautiful women in the world come from Thailand. Oprah says so."

"If Oprah says so I guess that ends the discussion," Peter said, glancing at his watch. The game was about to begin on television and he didn't want to miss the first inning. "As long as I don't have to deal with her; do whatever you want." He hurried into his den, turned on his big screen television and lit up his first cigar of the day.

It was about 11:30 the next morning when Peter finished weeding his vegetable garden. He put his tools away, stood admiring his tomatoes that were almost ripe enough to pick, and then headed up to the house with the idea of opening a 'cold one' and reading the morning paper. When he reached the top of the steps he heard voices and then saw Miriam leading someone by the hand across the deck toward him.

"Peter, come meet Maité. You know I told you all about her last night," Miriam gushed. Peter wiped his hands on his overalls and stepped out of the sun to greet their new employee. Her hair, which fell below her shoulders, was panther black. She had high cheekbones, slanting dark eyes, skin the color of a newborn fawn and a body wrapped tightly in a multicolored sarong that displayed little, but promised much.

"Bonjour, Monsieur." Her voice was deep and husky, arousing parts of Peter that had been in repose for many years. She offered him her hand and made a small curtsy. He took it in both of his own; it was firm and warm to his touch.

"I'm Peter," he said, mesmerized.

"She knows your name, Peter. Now go help unload her things from the station wagon, while I call Charlotte and tell her we have arrived safely," Miriam prattled on. Peter followed Maité out to the car as he was bid, blushing at the thoughts that were racing through his mind as his eyes focused upon a derriere the likes of which he had never seen except in the centerfold of *Playboy*.

When he had deposited the last pieces of luggage in their guest room, where she was planning to stay until he completed building the apartment over the garage, Maité said, "Merci, Monsieur Peter. I hope you will much like Maité. I very hard try to make happy Monsieur with me."

Peter could not believe what was happening to him. In the space of minutes this exotic young woman had turned his legs to jelly and sent his libido into orbit. He stood staring at her, his mind spinning fantasy scenarios that

would put a blush on the cheeks of a Babylon-
ian harlot.

"Monsieur?" she said, cocking her head to
the side and smiling. "I go help Madame now,
oui?"

"No, no, don't go. I mean yes, si, oui, of
course, it's only that, I was just . . ." Peter mumbled incoherently. Maité turned quickly and disappeared down the stairs. He slumped down on
the edge of the bed. There was a full-length mirror on the wall opposite where he was seated. He
glared at his image. Curly reddish-grey hair
formed a half halo around his freckled, sunburned, bald dome. His three-day growth of
beard fought with wrinkles for dominance of a
craggy face smudged with sweat and dirt from
the garden. Piercing blue eyes under red and grey
speckled brows gazed back at him.

"I look like an Irish Friar Tuck for chrissake," he muttered, pulling a Dodgers baseball
cap out of his back pocket and putting it on his
head to cover up his bald pate. When he leaned
closer and scrutinized his face he noticed some
grey hairs peeking out of his nose and ears. "That
can be fixed easily," he whispered aloud as he
bared his teeth. The two in the front were whiter
and brighter than his real teeth. That could be

fixed too. He stood up and sucked in his gut. Nothing changed. His belly continued to hang over his belt.

"What are you doing Peter?" Miriam flowed into the room. He whirled around like the time he had been caught by his mother doing something that would make him go blind.

"This was my mother's favorite mirror," he blurted senselessly, reaching over and straightening it one way and then the other.

"So what do you think?"

"About the mirror?" he asked foolishly.

"No, dummy, about Maité."

Peter felt stirrings in his nether parts with the mere mention of her name.

"Okay, I guess. Can she cook?"

"We were just discussing that. She's going to cook dinner for us tonight and serve it out on the patio. I happen to know that Estelle and Louis are having a cocktail party on their patio tonight to which we were not invited I might add, and there we will be on our patio which is at least ten feet longer than theirs, being served dinner by Maité, within spitting distance of their big deal affair." Miriam fished two Fanny Farmer chocolates out of her pocket and stuffed them in her mouth.

Peter began to work out at the club, had his
teeth fixed, and the hairs removed from his nose
and ears, and wore his baseball cap constantly.
On several occasions when he contrived to be in
the same space with Maité while Miriam was
away from the house, she managed to elude him
graciously. The more she put him off, the more
infatuated he became. He awakened in the morning thinking of her and spent the whole day trying to devise excuses to be near her. He dreamed
about her when his eyes were closed and when
they were open. On one occasion she came out
of the bathroom with only a towel wrapped
around her waist and he caught a glimpse of her
pert young breasts for an instant before she
ducked back into her room. He carried that
image around with him for days afterward, and
each night before he went to sleep he would
recreate the encounter in his mind and hope that
it would continue into his dreams.

He tried to engage her in conversation about
her life in Malaysia, but she would always reply,
"Is nothing interesting in Maité's life," flash him
a winning smile and hurry off to perform some
domestic task. Then one day when Peter had her
cornered in the kitchen, she turned to him and
said, "You like Maité, Monsieur Peter?"

He replied, "Like you? God, woman, can't
you tell that I am crazy about you, that I wor-
ship the ground you walk on?" He took a step
toward her, intending to take her in his arms
and smother her with kisses and whatever else
she might permit, but she slipped out of his grasp
and managed to put the kitchen table between
them. Peter's heart was racing. He knew that he
must have this woman or die.

"How much you like Maité?"

"So much I want to spend the rest of my life
with you. I want to marry you. I want to . . ."

"Marry?" she gasped.

"Yes, marry you and spend the rest of my life
as your servant."

"You make fun with me, no?" she said, holding her hands over her ears.

"No, Maité, I have never been more serious
in my life," he declared solemnly. She stared at
him wide-eyed and then ran up to her room. He
followed after her and pounded on her bedroom
door, but she wouldn't open it.

A few days later when she was peeling vegetables at the kitchen sink he came up behind her
and put his arms around her waist. She didn't
turn away as she had in the past. He moved
closer, thrusting himself against her. She gave a

barely audible whimper and moved her hips ever so slightly back and forth.

"Oh my God," Peter gasped.

"Peter," Miriam called as she slammed the back door and headed toward the kitchen.

"Peter, where are you, I want you to carry in an antique end table I just bought." Maité rushed out of the kitchen, leaving Peter frustrated and angrier with Miriam than he had ever been before. He started after Maité, thought better of it and waited for Miriam.

"Didn't you hear me, Peter? I said I bought an end table for the guest room and I want you to carry it up for me."

"Screw the guest room. Miriam, I want to talk to you."

"What are you all bent out of shape about?"

"I want out, Miriam. I want out as soon as possible."

"Out of what, Peter?" she answered opening up the refrigerator and removing a carton of ice cream. "You're not making any sense, as usual." She scooped out a large portion of butter pecan in a bowl. Peter watched her every move but didn't say another word until she flopped down on the stool at the kitchen table. Her legs were spread apart because her thighs were so fat she couldn't touch her knees together. Peter observed that her buttocks hung over the stool on all sides. His memory of the look and the feel of Maité's slim waist obliterated all else in his mind.

"I want a divorce, Miriam," he blurted. He could feel the blood rushing to his head.

"And I want to take a trip to Mars," she replied between spoonsful of ice cream.

"I'm serious, Miriam." He sputtered the words through clenched teeth.

"So am I, Peter. What's your problem? Have you found a bimbo to play with? It is another woman, I suppose."

"Yes Miriam, it is another woman."

"Well I don't want to know who it is. Just tell me when you are planning to move out of the house," Miriam said, returning to the refrigerator for another helping of ice cream.

"I don't think you are taking me seriously, Miriam."

"Of course I am. You said you want a divorce. That's fine by me. When it gets all sorted out I'll be rich, and you will be broke." She laughed.

"I don't care about money. You can have the money and the end tables and the silverware and anything else you want except the house."

"You certainly don't expect me to give up my home so that you and your bimbo can play in my sandbox, do you?"

"For God's sake Miriam, I told you I'll give you everything, but this house is—"

"Forget it, Peter. Where's Maité? Dinner is supposed to be ready by six o'clock. I'm starved."

"Eat, eat, eat. That's all you ever think of."

"Sex, sex, sex. That's all you ever think of," she countered.

Peter spent the night at the Holiday Inn. He calculated his net worth and his life expectancy and decided that he was going to have Maité whatever it cost. "What good is money without happiness, without Maité?" he asked aloud. Those few moments of ecstasy with Maité in the kitchen before Miriam showed up were the most exhilarating he could recall in his lifetime, and he had just scratched the surface of what their life would be like together. She was so young and beautiful. She made him feel like a young bull. He thought of that gorgeous body lying beside him every night for the rest of his life. If she hadn't responded to him it would be different, but she had! She hadn't run away from him. She had wiggled her little bottom for him and heightened his passion to a fever pitch. "What do I need a lot of money for?" he asked himself. "All I need is enough so Maité and I can go to Malaysia and buy a little cottage beside the sea. I've got income from my half of the trust fund, and in seven years I'll have my Social Security. Enough to live like royalty in Malaysia."

He returned home the next day and moved into the unfinished apartment over the garage. Whenever he attempted to caress Maité she pushed him away, saying, "No! Monsieur is still married. Monsieur marry Maité first. When I am Mrs. Doyle, then I do everything to please Monsieur Peter." She always left him hungrier than ever with desire. The doubts he had about surrendering everything to Miriam in exchange for his freedom were slowly being buried in an avalanche of lust.

It took two months for the lawyers to work things out. Peter was shocked to discover that the trust he had created in Miriam's name alone, to avoid paying a large capital gains tax, could not be broken, but he managed to wheedle some cash for himself out of the settlement which would be enough to buy his dream cottage in Malaysia and an exotic honeymoon in Fiji to boot. Until his Social Security benefits kicked in they would live off the six hundred dollar monthly annuity that Miriam had finally conceded to him when he signed over the house to her.

Within hours after the divorce decree was granted, a justice of the peace married Peter and Maité. They drove directly to the Los Angeles airport and boarded a plane headed to Fiji for their honeymoon. Peter spent his wedding night sleeping fitfully on the plane, unable to distinguish between his dreams and the fantasies he harbored in his half-sleep. "Just a few more hours," he whispered, kissing Maité's cheek.

As soon as they passed through customs, a sprightly old man with a wondrous smile approached them.

"Mr. Doyle?" he asked timidly.

"Indeed, that's me and who might you be?" Peter inquired, not unkindly.

"Me Tonto. Ni sa yadra—that means good morning. Lako mai—Come with me . . . to Lazy Moon Beach Hotel, yes?"

"Don't see why not." Peter replied affably. "Is Tonto your first name or do I call you Mr. Tonto?"

"First name, last name, all same. Don't you know Lone Ranger?"

Tonto led them to his battered station wagon which ran well enough to get them to the

Lazy Moon Beach Hotel. It consisted of a few thatched-roof cottages snuggled into a hill surrounding a small lagoon. When Maité stepped out of the dilapidated old taxi and gazed around her, she clapped her hands and cried, "C'est magnifique!"

Peter beckoned for her to watch him sign the register as Peter and Maité Doyle. "Maité Doyle. Sounds queer, doesn't it, Mrs. Doyle?" he asked.

"Mais non, Cherie, I think is magnifique, everything is magnifique." She laughed her wonderful low, throaty, sensual laugh.

After their luggage was delivered to the cottage and they had a chance to survey their lodgings, Maité exclaimed, "I'm starving, Cherie." She dragged Peter down to the dining terrace, where they had several potent tropical drinks and conch fritters. When they finished Peter said, "Well, how about we take a little siesta, Mrs. Doyle?" rolling his eyes skyward and smiling his most mischievous smile.

"I go swim first," Maité answered sweetly, taking him by the hand and leading him back to their cottage.

"Monsieur . . . I mean my husband . . . take nice sleep, save energy for tonight." She blushed and began searching through her luggage. Although he was disappointed, Peter lay back on the bed with his hands clasped behind his head, willing to settle for watching her change into her bathing suit. Maité pulled out a one-piece white swimsuit, held it up for him to see, and then darted into the bathroom. He thought that her modesty was clearly a virtue, but he was insane with desire to consummate their marriage. "We've been married for almost eighteen hours and I ain't even seen her knickers yet," he lamented, as he dozed off waiting for her to emerge from the bathroom.

When he awakened, the evening's first star was visible in the sky. He looked at his watch. It was 10:30 in the evening. "Can't be," he exclaimed as he crawled off the bed. "I must have slept over eight hours. What a stupid way to begin a honeymoon," Then he spied her note: *"Sleepy head, I go to bar. Maité."* He rubbed his chin and felt the stubble of grey beard. He hated how old he looked when he was unshaven, and had vowed that Maité should never see him that way. He hurried into the bathroom to shave and shower. There was no hot water. "Three hundred dollars a day and no hot water for chrissake," he cursed. The afternoon sun had beaten into the bedroom, which felt like a sauna, and by the time he was dressed and on his way down to the bar his shirt was already soaked with perspiration. As he hurried along the winding path he heard Maité's Lauren Bacall laugh and followed the sound. She was seated at the bar surrounded by three very handsome young Fiji men. They were speaking in French, which Peter didn't begin to understand, but he understood very well the sparkle in Maité's eyes as she gazed on the beautiful torsos of the young men who were all naked to the waist. He was shocked to see Maité holding up a cigarette to be lit (he thought she was a non-smoker) and then playfully blowing smoke into the face of the young man who had lit it for her. She was wearing a flimsy dress which barely covered her breasts and she was showing more leg than he himself had ever seen. At that moment she looked up and saw him. "Bon soir, Cherie," she exclaimed, as she slid off the bar stool and walked unsteadily toward him. She was barefoot and ravishing. Even without shoes she was almost a head taller than he. She took off his baseball cap ceremoniously and kissed him on his bald pate. He turned crimson, grabbed his cap away from her and jammed it back on his head. She took his arm and steered him to the bar.

"Here is sleepy-head husband of me," she said, laughing. Her new friends joined in the laughter. "Sleepy-head," they repeated, then they all stepped forward to shake Peter's hand. He had never felt more miserable in his life.

"Drink?" one of the young men asked, moving his thumbs-up fist toward his mouth in a drinking motion.

"Oui, oui. Gin, much ice," Maité called out to the bartender. When the drink was made and delivered into Peter's hand, everyone cheered.

He gulped the drink down and they all applauded. Within seconds he had another drink in his hand. He began to feel better. Maité was staying close to him and not paying any attention to anyone else. Peter relaxed and began to enjoy himself. A guitarist showed up and all the young men started to sing. Peter bought a round of drinks and soon the party had expanded to include everyone in the bar. Two men and a young woman began to dance to a pair of drums that materialized out of nowhere. Then Maité danced alone. Within moments the room was hushed. It was the most erotic performance Peter had ever seen, and the crowd went wild when she finished. Peter bought another round for the bar and did his own solo dance which was a mixture of jitterbug and ballet. He brought down the house and ordered another round. At 2 A.M. Peter passed out and was carried back to their cottage under Maité's supervision. After she had undressed him and tucked him in bed, she rejoined the party.

When Peter awakened the next morning he thought the Third Marine Division was engaged in war games inside his head. His mouth tasted as if he had licked the urinal in the men's room at Grand Central Station. He moaned audibly.

"Aha! It eez alive, no?" Maité teased.

"No, I'm dead, or I wish I were," he wailed.

"Drink this," she commanded.

"What is it?" he asked feebly.

"Mary's blood."

"Oh no . . . no . . . no!"

"Is good. Drink and you live, not die."

After two Bloody Marys and a bowl of chicken soup that made his eyes water, Peter was willing to get up and cautiously join the living. During his recuperation Maité voiced her displeasure with everything. She complained about the heat and the humidity, the lack of hot water and air-conditioning. She bemoaned the fact that she was missing Oprah and the soaps; and said that the food was "primitif." "Chicken,

chicken, chicken. Yuch! I want Big Mac, and pizza with pepperoni," she pouted. Peter nursed his headache and sulked.

By the time they had eaten dinner by candlelight, with the sound and the smell of jasmine and the sea surrounding them, he was feeling normal again. Maité continued to complain about everything but he didn't pay any attention to her, because it was getting late, and from the moment his hangover had begun to diminish he could only think about his conjugal rights as the husband of this gorgeous young woman.

They walked slowly, hand in hand, from the dining terrace to their cottage. There wasn't enough movement of air to stir a single leaf. The heat and humidity were so oppressive it was like strolling through a sauna fully clothed. As they labored up the long steep winding walkway to their cottage, Peter thought that it would be just his luck to have a heart attack and die before they reached it. When they entered the cottage it was stifling. Maité sighed and turned on the overhead fan. Peter was breathing heavily, but, he was determined.

" I need bath and cognac. Maybe husband please go bar, get cognac."

"Okay, I could use a stiff something myself."

He laughed at his own joke. Maité waited until he left and then she disrobed and walked slowly into the bathroom.

When he returned with the liquor the shower was still running. He sat down in the only chair in the room and stared out the open window. The waves caressed the beach, splashed with silver from the rising moon. He heard the tinkling of the loose coral at the water's edge each time a wave raced back to sea to regroup for another gentle rush up the beach.

He wondered if he should get undressed and lie down on the bed and wait for her, but then he looked down at his sagging belly and remembered the young men at the bar. "What the hell have I got myself into? I'm thirty-three years older than she is," he grumbled. As they walked side by side back to the cottage he had been aroused, but now he had no feeling at all. "Perhaps when I finally see her undressed—what the hell is she doing in there?" Then the bathroom door opened and there she was, gorgeous . . . smiling . . . makeup in place . . . wearing a white silk high-neck Mandarin gown with tiny gold carved buttons down the front from the top of the collar to the bottom of the floor-length skirt.

"You like?" she asked, as she twirled

around. He started to speak but the words got caught in his throat. He swallowed. "You are beautiful, so beautiful," he whispered. She came to him and they kissed. He stood on tiptoes. It was a long lingering kiss. He knew at last it would be all right . . . the best . . . worth all the sacrifices . . . the waiting . . . the longing . . . the tantalizing agony. He reached up and caressed her, while their lips were still joined, with tongues exploring . . . nibbling . . . juices flowing. He started to fumble with the buttons at her bodice.

"No, Cherie, let me," she whispered in his ear and then led him over to the easy chair. She turned on her portable tape deck. It was his favorite Nat King Cole recording.

Unforgettable, that's what you are . . . Unforgettable. . . .

She started to sway back and forth to the music and slowly began to unbutton her gown. Peter sat mesmerized as she cupped one breast and then the other, caressing each of them as she continued to open the collar and then the bodice. She let her hands slide down to her hips.

Peter was silently counting the buttons as they parted. "Twenty-seven . . . twenty-eight . . ." He guessed there were one-hundred buttons from top to bottom. "Thirty." When she undid the thirty-first button she shrugged her shoulders. Peter gasped when the top of her gown fell to her waist exposing her small, perfectly shaped breasts with large thrusting nipples. He started to get out of his chair and come to her. He couldn't hold back any longer, but Maité stepped quickly to kneel in front of him, encouraging him to kiss and caress them. Peter grabbed her gown, intending to rip it off but she slipped out of his grasp.

"Non, non, non!" she hissed. "Not like animal."

Peter was beside himself. She was driving him crazy. He had never felt such compelling passion and desire in all his life.

"Please Maité, please. I can't stand it any longer," he begged.

That's why darling it's regrettable. . . .

She turned her back on him and began to unbutton her gown again. She was making little whimpering sounds and he could see the perspiration glistening on her unblemished slender cocoa-colored flesh.

Then she whirled around to face him . . . defiantly . . . hands on her hips . . . long shapely legs spread apart. . . . "Voila, Monsieur!"

"Eeeeeeeeahhhhh—" Peter screamed and lost consciousness.

Maité checked his pulse. It was strong. By the time she had changed into a pair of jeans and a tank top, Peter had started to come around, and began to moan. She handed him a tall cognac. He took a hefty swig, keeping his eyes fixed on her the while, as if she might turn into a witch if he blinked.

"Are you playing a trick on me or are you a MAN?" he hissed.

"I no play trick and I no man." Maité replied forcefully.

"But you've got a . . ."

"Just like you, yes?"

"Yeah, dammit, just like me. Only . . . Jesus, what about the breasts?" Peter stammered.

"Silicon."

"Oh my God, I'm married to a . . . a . . . TRANSVESTITE! Can you hear me, Miriam, I'm married to a fucking transvestite," he screamed.

"You got bad mouth, Peter. I not a fooking transvestite, I am . . . transgendered."

"What the hell's the difference?" Peter snarled.

"I'm no freak. God fooked me up. I am beautiful woman. You say I am beautiful woman. You say you love me. We marry. You tell me over and over that I make you happier than any other woman in your life. I have one small problem, easy fix. Give me money so surgeon make me total woman."

"I don't have any money," Peter snarled.

"Ha ha. You can't fool me. Madame tell me you millionaire."

"Ha ha yourself. I gave Miriam all my money so I could marry you. "

"No, mon dieu, no, no!" Maité gasped. "Why you think I marry old man? I need money to be total woman." Maité sat down on the bed and cried, then she began to laugh hysterically.

"What's so God-damned funny?" Peter demanded.

"Is crazy. You marry me to get something which you think I have, but I don't. I marry you so I can get the money I think you have . . . but you don't. You gave up the money to get the thing you wanted which I haven't got but wish I had and could get if I had the money."

"It's called poetic justice," Peter said, shrugging his shoulders dejectedly. "Okay, so we're stuck with each other. We'll just have to go to Malaysia and work things out from there."

"Malaysia? No way Hosay. I work all my life to get out of Malaysia. I no go back. Never! We go to California. No more talk. Sleep now. Talk tomorrow." She/he stood up, and took off her/his tank top. Peter looked at her/his lovely body.

"Maité?" he said softly.

"Oui," she/he replied cautiously.

"How much would it cost to make you a total woman?"

Chapter Nine

BETH WENT TO THE HEAD OF THE stairs and called down to the game room. "Okay guys, dinner's ready." As they climbed the stairs, Michael had his arm draped around Doc's shoulder. "No, I won't take a promissory note, I want the twelve bucks right now," Doc said forcefully. When they reached the top of the steps, Michael said, "Will you lend me twelve bucks, Beth? Your husband insists upon being paid his winnings right now and I don't have a penny with me. I'm good for it, I promise."

"Yeah, yeah, I've heard that before, and until a half hour ago I would probably have given it to you, but after reading about your friend Maité, I don't know, Mike. . . ."

"Really awful, hey Hon?" Doc chuckled. "That figures. The first three stories he gave us were probably ghost-written."

"I'm looking at you from a totally different perspective from now on O'Leary, and I'm not sure I want you hanging around my husband either."

"You said there was some sex in this one, right?" Doc asked.

"Sort of," Michael said sheepishly, glancing at Beth.

"That explains it. Women are great when it comes to the theory of sex, it's the practice of it that has them befuddled."

"Right on!" Michael chimed in.

"You two adolescents deserve each other," Beth said, leading them into the dinning room.

"I'm willing to dump him if you'll read another story, Beth," Michael said.

"Spoken like a true friend of the nineties," Doc sighed.

"Sorry old man, business is business." Michael ambled back to the foyer and retrieved the story entitled *Spatsco* from his briefcase. "What am I bid?" he sang, holding the envelope aloft.

"A piece of homemade pumpkin pie with real whipped cream on top," Beth offered.

"Sold!" Michael smiled and handed her the envelope.

Chapter Ten

Spatsco

"I need you to fix my machine, Jim, it's skipping again."

"I'll get to you as soon as I can," Jim Duffy answered without looking up from his work bench. "If I don't get this conveyor belt fixed, nobody is going to be able to do anything today. It's the third time this week it's broken down. The patches are larger than the belt."

"I don't know how you do it, Jim, keeping these old machines running year after year. Do you think old Foggybottom will ever let loose a few bucks to get us some new equipment?"

"It's not just that the machines are falling apart, I've seen stuff in the catalogues that could put out our product ten times as fast with about one quarter of the work force."

"Jeez, I hope you didn't tell the old man about that or I'll be out of a job."

"That's the whole point, Sue. He wouldn't need me either," Jim replied.

"Not true, there is no way in hell he could run this plant without you."

"That's what I like to hear," he said affably.

Sue shook her head. "Don't underestimate yourself, Jim."

He shrugged his shoulders and smiled at her. They had worked together on the shop floor for over ten years. Jim took a final turn with his wrench to tighten the old leather belt and then pulled the power switch and put the belt in gear.

"Now let's see what's wrong with that old relic of yours so you can get back to work instead of standing around gabbing with me," he said, putting an arm around her shoulders and leading her back to her work station. Just as he started to take the machine apart, he was called on the intercom. He walked over to his battered desk in the corner of the big workroom, put the receiver to one ear and clapped his hand over the other in order to block out the noise.

"What's up, Fran?"

"Mr. Greystone wants to see you in his office right away."

"Can't come right now. I got a machine down, might take me twenty minutes or so to get it running again, then I'll be up," Jim said pleasantly.

"Hold on, let me check with him," Fran said. Jim glanced around the floor. With the exception of Sue's machine everything seemed to be running smoothly. Jim sighed contentedly as he waited. He enjoyed the sight, the sound and the smell of the old plant. Fran came back on the line.

"He says he doesn't care how many machines are working, he wants you up here now!"

"Okay, he's the boss. I'll be right up," Jim replied. He pulled a rag out of his back pocket, wiped the grease off his hands and headed for the stairs leading up to Greystone's office. As he passed Sue's station he said, "Might as well take a coffee break, sweetheart, the Old Man wants me for something." Jim climbed the narrow stairs and walked down the familiar hallway almost the full length of the building before reaching the administrative offices.

"Hi Jim. Go right on in."

"What's up, Fran?"

"I'm not real sure. Maybe you and I can talk after you speak with Mr. Greystone."

"What's the matter?"

"I don't know . . . something is going on but I don't know what. Come see me later, okay?"

"Sure thing."

Jim knocked once and opened the door into the office of the president of the Greystone Spats Company. When he entered the spacious, well-appointed office, Greystone got up from behind the massive executive desk and came forward to greet his oldest employee. Greystone was a short man wearing a banker's dark blue suit, dazzling white shirt, club tie and Rotary pin in his lapel. "Good morning, Duffy, come in. How about a cup of coffee, or would you prefer a whiskey?"

"Whiskey?" Jim said, raising his eyebrows. "It's only 8:30 in the morning. I've never had a drink of whiskey in the morning in my whole life." He brushed off his coveralls as he eased into the plush high back chair which Greystone indicated.

"I'm sure that's true, but today is different. It has been one hundred and three years since the Greystone Spats Company was founded by Grandpa Clarence in 1894. Did you know that, Duffy?"

"I should, workin' here all these years and all, but I can't say as how I did," Jim said nervously.

"Would you believe that some people don't even know what a pair of spats is . . . are?"

"Yes sir, I do know that. Sometimes I wish we made boots, if you don't mind my saying so. I get kidded a lot, all in good fun . . . still . . . ."

"I know exactly what you mean, Duffy, but you don't have to think about it anymore. We are going to close our doors tomorrow and then we can all go fishing."

"I don't get your drift, sir. What do you mean we're closin' our doors tomorrow?" Jim asked, glancing anxiously at the half empty whiskey glass sitting on Greystone's desk. "I don't understand."

"You see, Duffy, it really began a few years after you came to work for the company. How long have you been with us?" Greystone demanded.

"Over forty years, Mr. Greystone. I began to work here right off the farm in 1955. It was my first job. I was eighteen years old then," Jim said proudly.

"Forty years . . . Just think of it Duffy: Eight hours a day, five days a week, fifty weeks a year for forty years."

"Eighty thousand hours, give or take a few," Jim offered. "I have been involved in the production of better than five million pairs of spats from 1955 until now," Jim responded.

"Indeed you have, Duffy. But now we must talk about the future. I brought you in here this morning to talk about your retirement."

"Retirement?" Jim blurted out. "I can't retire. I have to work here seven more years."

"Why is that?"

"Me and Essie have a plan, but we got to save up another seven years, till I'm sixty-five."

"I'm sorry Duffy, that's impossible." Greystone said forcefully. "Tomorrow morning the Greystone Spats Company will close its doors for good."

"But you can't do that. I won't turn sixty-five for another seven years. I mean Essie and me have been saving up to buy one of them manufactured homes down near Daytona Beach in a real nice development there. It's called Bear Creek, and it's got a clubhouse and a pool and shuffleboard, and . . . but we won't be able to do any of that unless we both go on working until I'm sixty-five."

"Oh, it will all work out, I'm sure. You'll be able to find another job between now and then, don't worry."

"Don't worry . . . what do you mean 'don't worry?' I'm fifty-eight years old and I don't know how to do anything except make spats. We'll never make it," Jim said, panicking.

"Of course you will. That's always been your problem, Duffy. You don't have any vision. You worry about the small stuff. Think big for once in your life."

"That's easy for you to say. I don't mean to be disrespectful, sir, but you're the president of the company, you work with your head. I'm a factory worker, I work with my hands."

"But after all these years, you must have learned *something* from me about how to make decisions. Listen to me, Duffy, think the way I do. Think the way Management thinks, not the way Labor thinks."

"I'll try to do that," Jim said, shrugging his shoulders in defeat. He knew the old man would never understand.

"Good man. Now listen carefully to me, Duffy. Do you know how much money we have in the Greystone Trust at this very moment?" Greystone pulled a sheet of paper out of the top drawer of his desk and placed it ceremoniously on top of the great leather ledger.

"No sir, I wouldn't have any way of knowing that. I'm a shop-worker not a bookkeeper," Jim replied testily.

Ignoring the rebuff, Greystone continued. "I checked with the bank just before it closed yesterday afternoon and confirmed that the lines on the graph have crossed. We have arrived at the day of reckoning. That's what it all means."

"I'm sorry Mr. Greystone, but frankly, I don't know what you're talking about."

"Of course you don't, because I have kept the secret of this company all to myself." Greystone leaned back in his chair. "You see, in 1887 Grandpa began to put ten-percent of the company's earnings in an investment trust account every year. He must have seen the depression coming, because just before he died in 1927, he sold all of the stocks and bonds in the investment account and bought gold and then put a clause in his will which declared that as long as there was money in the trust fund, the company must continue to operate whether we made a profit or not. He figured that the money in the fund really belonged to the employees, but in his view of things they weren't capable of investing it wisely. He also believed that if a man was willing to work, there should always be a job for him. This all took place before anyone ever heard of Social

Security, you understand. In any event, we were hit hard like everyone else by the depression, and never really recovered after that. But the investment trust fund had grown dramatically over the years and when Grandpa died my father took over the management of the company. Daddy never touched that gold until December 31, 1941. On that day he personally escorted every ounce of it down to Washington, D.C., and delivered it to the Secretary of the United States Treasury and exchanged it all for World War II savings bonds. They quoted him in *The Wall Street Journal* when he said, 'Hell, if America doesn't win the war what good is the gold?'

"After the war Daddy reinvested in the big companies that were making America the greatest nation on earth. Unfortunately the Greystone company stopped making a profit years ago. Since then we've been living off the trust fund. We haven't sold more than a few thousand pairs of spats since the early fifties."

"But, but . . ." Jim stammered, "What happened to the five million pairs of spats we have produced since then?"

"They're in our warehouse. And you're right, we have just over five million pairs of spats stored there. But I'll find a way to get rid of them after we close down," Greystone declared jovially.

Jim slumped down in his chair and spoke just above a whisper. "It's a joke. I have devoted my life to a joke. For forty years I have worried about every last pair of spats that went out the door. It was my job to make sure that every stitch was perfect, the buttons all uniform, making certain that we were producing a first-quality product, but it was all just a joke." Jim was fighting to hold back the tears.

"It wasn't a joke on you. The trust fund kept us all going for the forty years you have worked here. It paid our rent and sent our kids, yours and mine, to college, right up until today, when our liabilities exactly equal our assets."

At that moment Greystone's secretary Fran burst into the room.

"Mr. Greystone," she exclaimed, "there's a big guy out here who says he's supposed to pick up my typewriter." Greystone jumped up and hurried out to his secretary's office. "Oh for goodness sakes, wait a minute, mister, it's not time yet."

"Who are you?" The burly moving man asked.

"I'm president of the company. You're not

due to come until 9:00 on the 15th. Today is only the 5th."

"My orders say pick up the stuff at 9 A.M. today." The mover offered a document to Greystone who glanced at it briefly.

"I'll take care of this," Greystone said as he grabbed the phone. . . . "The phone is dead," he exclaimed, holding the receiver out in front of him as if it were a dead rat. Then the lights flickered and went out.

"Damn! All this isn't scheduled until the 15th," Greystone said. Then he retreated into his office, picked up his cell phone and called the mover and the telephone and power companies and blamed the mistake on the computer.

"Fran, tell Michael to blow the noon whistle and then pass the word that there is an important meeting in fifteen minutes. Now, Duffy, come back into my office and shut the door please."

"I think I'll take that whiskey now if you don't mind, Mr. Greystone."

"Sure. Here you go." Greystone poured a small drink and handed it to Jim.

"I'm sorry, Mr. Greystone, I don't understand what's going on." Jim said, grimacing as he took a sip of the whiskey.

Greystone settled back in his big leather chair. "Well there was no reason for you people down in the shop to understand it. Now listen. Grandpa decreed that the company must produce a minimum of three hundred pairs of spats every day, five days a week, fifty weeks a year."

"And we did exactly that," Jim responded. "That has been our goal. Fifteen hundred pairs of spats a week no matter what, and we only failed once when the whole plant came down with the Asian flu in 1969, and even then we all worked overtime for free afterwards to make up for the time we lost. Do you remember that, Mr. Greystone?"

"I sure do, Duffy, and I was very proud of all of you."

"But now you are telling me it was all for nothing. I have devoted forty years to no purpose at all. I have spent my whole life blowing air into a paper bag."

"Not true, not true at all," Greystone countered. "Grandpa determined that it took exactly thirty-two dedicated employees to produce three hundred pairs of spats a day, so he directed that as long as there was money in the trust fund, thirty-two loyal workers would be employed here until the day that the debts of the company, including severance pay for all employees, exactly equaled the assets of the company, and that will happen today!"

"Severance pay?" Jim perked up, hoping something might be salvaged from the tragedy he perceived.

"Now that's the wonderful part of it, Duffy. Every employee will get severance pay based upon their length of service to the company. In your case I think it amounts to six weeks' pay."

"Six weeks' pay? That's my reward for devoting forty years to the company and accomplishing nothing in my life?" Jim sputtered, pounding his fists on the arms of his chair. Then he stood up and walked grim-faced over to the window and stared down at the Lonesome Cafe, where he had eaten lunch every weekday since he was eighteen years old. When he regained his composure he said, "I must have drunk over 4250 cups of Jemma's coffee."

"What's that, Duffy?" Greystone asked.

"Nothing important, Mr. Greystone, I was just wondering what will happen to Jemma Sulzberger when we're not here anymore to drink her coffee and eat her homemade pie."

"Who's Jemma Sulzberger?"

"She owns the Lonesome Cafe across the street. You must know old Jemma," Jim said incredulously. "All these years . . . " Jim came back and sat across the desk from Greystone. "Tell me, Mr. Greystone, if us workers down in the shop have spent all our lives making millions of pairs of spats that nobody wanted, what have you been doing every day for the past forty years?"

"Well now," Greystone replied haughtily, "I negotiated contracts, paid the suppliers, attended business conventions. I have a Chamber of Commerce lunch meeting on Tuesday, Rotary on Wednesday, Kiwanis Club on Thursday. Is it any wonder that I don't know who Jane Schultz is?"

"Jemma Sulzberger," Jim mumbled.

"And let me remind all of you that I'm the one who personally signs all of your paychecks every week."

"But for God's sake, Mr. Greystone, why didn't you just shut down the damn plant forty years ago, and let us do something with our lives instead of—I can't believe it." Jim wailed. "It must have cost millions to keep this place going for all these years with only a few pairs of spats being sold each year?"

"Well, actually we have continued to sell more than a few pairs over the years." Greystone countered. "Remember when we supplied one hundred pairs of crimson spats to the King of Siam for his honor guard?"

"Yes, but surely that was not enough reason to keep the plant open all these years. I mean, a few hundred pairs a year . . . such a waste."

Greystone leaned forward and spoke in a conspiratorial voice. "Duffy, Duffy, don't you get it? If I hadn't spent the money exactly the way I was instructed under the will, the whole trust fund would have been paid over to the remaindermen!"

"The remaindermen? Who the hell are they?" Jim demanded, emboldened by the whiskey.

"Dozens of my distant relatives nobody ever heard of. Just think of it Duffy, $20 million would have been paid over to a bunch of strangers. Wasn't it better that I fed the employees of the Greystone Spats Company?"

"I think my life has been a total loss," Jim moaned.

"No, no, no! "Greystone exclaimed, becoming exasperated. "Don't you see? Your life would not have been one whit different if we had sold every darn pair of spats you made. You were paid every week, you got a cost of living raise every year just as the covenant required. What was your salary when you started with the Company?"

"Sixty-one dollars and sixty-six cents a week," Jim mumbled.

"And now?" Greystone asked.

"Four hundred thirteen dollars and twelve cents." Jim answered.

"Do you realize that over the years, the company has paid you . . . come look at this, Duffy," Greystone commanded, opening up the massive ledger book and running his finger down a long column of handwritten entries. "Five hundred thirty-nine thousand, eight hundred twenty-two dollars and seventeen cents. Just think of it Duffy: over a half million dollars. That's a lot of money!"

"It was a lot of my life . . . for no purpose."

"You keep saying 'no purpose, no purpose.' What do you think the purpose of life is anyway? The purpose of life is to live, for goodness sake. What more could you have expected? Now look here, Duffy." Greystone opened his desk drawer and pulled out a large bundle of envelopes. "Here it is. This is yours." Greystone handed over an envelope with Jim's name neatly typed across the front. Jim took the envelope and just stared at it.

"Well, open it." Greystone commanded. Jim

meticulously opened the envelope and withdrew a letter. "Read it to me please Duffy."

Jim rummaged in his pocket and retrieved a pair of wire-rimmed eyeglasses with a piece of adhesive tape holding one of the lenses in place.

"Dear Mr. Duffy,

Enclosed please find a check in the amount of $2,460.00. Congratulations for a job well done."

Very truly yours,
Clarence Greystone III, President

"Just think of it," Greystone beamed. "Two thousand four hundred sixty dollars. Six weeks salary."

"So this is it," Jim said, staring at the letter.

"This is it, Duffy. The end of the Greystone road, so to speak. But such a happy ending. wouldn't you say?"

"I don't know what to say, Mr. Greystone," Jim mumbled, folding the letter and the check and putting them in his pocket.

"In order to keep this whole thing secret, I personally wrote every letter by hand, ran all the severance checks through the computer myself. Besides, I had the bank certify every single check

so that none of the employees will have any difficulty cashing these big checks. That money is
yours to do with whatever you wish. No one can
take that away from you no matter what. I've
thought of everything, Duffy."

"Did you get a severance check, too, Mr.
Greystone?"

"Not yet, but I will," Greystone said. "The
will treats me just like every other employee,
except I come last. What's left over comes to me."

"And the building, Mr. Greystone, how does
that figure in here?"

"Well now, Duffy, that's really a private executive matter, but between you and me the proceeds from the sale of the building—which I don't
really consider to be a company asset because it's
not what you would call a liquid asset, you see—
will come to me as a sort of a perk, for giving my
life to the company, don't you know."

"With its location right across from the
post office and next to city hall, it ought to be
worth a couple million, wouldn't you say, Mr.
Greystone?"

"At least," Greystone replied with a smile.

"I guess I should leave now," Jim said. Then
he got up from his chair and walked slowly to
the door.

"Good luck and God bless," Greystone pronounced, as Jim closed the door behind him.

"What's going on Jim?" Fran asked with a look of deep concern. "Did he forget to send out the checks for the electric bill and the phone bill?" she asked.

"No, I don't think so. Goodbye, Fran."

"Jim, where are you going?"

"I'm going home, Fran," Jim said softly. Then he walked out of the waiting room, down the wooden steps, and out the door. He shuffled across the parking lot to his battered 1985 Dodge Dart and then turned around to stare back at the old brick building where he had worked all his life. After a while he shrugged his shoulders and slipped in behind the wheel. He just sat there dazed for a long while, and then he pulled the letter and the check out of his pocket. He reread the letter and glanced at the check for the first time. "Jesus!" He exclaimed, and jumped out of the car to go back to Greystone's office. He took a few steps, hesitated and then returned to his car. It started up on the first turn of the key as it always did. He drove home slowly, stopping at the liquor store to buy a bottle of inexpensive champagne.

When Essie got seriously injured working at

the Whitesall Laundry Company two years ear-
lier, they cut her down to twenty hours a week.
She worked the early shift and was at home when
Jim arrived.

"Are you sick, Jim?" she asked, when he
walked in the door.

"Nah, I'm just fine, Essie."

"Then what in the world are you doing
home at this hour of the day?"

"It's a long story, love, I'll tell you all about
it in a minute. But first tell me, how much money
have we got in our dream house savings account?

"With last week's deposit I'd say around
$27,000. Why?"

"And when is our lease up on this place?"

"Next month. The new lease is on your desk
waiting for you to sign. What's this all about,
Jim?" she asked anxiously.

"Hold on now, just hold on, I have an idea
and I need to know all the facts."

"You and your ideas. The last idea you had
was investing in that Amway home sales scheme
that was going to make us millionaires. It cost us
over five hundred dollars and we still have three
cases of toilet paper, a carton of Kleenex, and ten
gallons of detergent in the basement."

"Good Lord, Essie, do you have to bring that

up every other day of my life? It was a mistake, I admitted it was a mistake, but in the long run it won't have cost us a dime."

"That's true if we live to be eighty or get the runs on a regular basis."

Jim smiled in spite of himself. "But this is different. I want you to start packing because we are going on a trip."

"Oh, we are, are we? Well let me tell you something, Mr. Rockerfeller, you're not getting a penny of our savings for no trip, so unless you won the lottery, forget it."

"Why do you always have to take the fun out of everything, Essie? I don't understand it. I'm not in the house five minutes and we're in an argument. Now listen to me for once. We are going on a trip and maybe we're coming back and maybe we ain't. The kids are all gone, your sister has moved to California, and your Friday night bowling team can get along without you. I'm not going to take your damn savings, so get your butt upstairs and start packing."

"Why do we always have to do things your way?" Essie complained, but she headed up the stairs anyway. It had only happened a few times in their many years of marriage, but she recognized the look in Jim's eyes and knew he wasn't going to back off. She also knew that sooner or later she would get it all straightened out. "But what the devil is he up to and where is he getting the money?" she wondered.

Jim sat down at his desk and pulled the phone book out of the top drawer. He checked the number twice and then dialed.

"Gulliver's Travel, may I help you?"

"Yes ma'am, I want two tickets to Daytona Beach, and I want to leave tomorrow morning."

When the travel arrangements were completed, Jim went upstairs to help Essie with the packing and fill her in on the plan.

"I didn't mean to be so mysterious, Essie," he said as he started to empty out his dresser drawers. "But you see, I still haven't made up my mind about the whole thing. I've got to think it through."

"It's not fair Jim. I don't know where we're going, I don't know how you're going to pay for it, I don't know how long we are going to be away, I don't even know whether to pack winter clothes or summer clothes. It's just not fair." Essie started to cry.

"Now, now, Jesus, don't start crying. You're right." And then he told Essie almost the whole story. He pulled out the letter and showed it to her. When she finished reading it she said. "You must be out of your mind. You've lost your job. Lord knows when you'll get another one at your age, and if you think we're going to spend that twenty-four hundred dollars on a trip, you've got another think coming, mister." Jim gently took the letter from her without saying a word, then he turned, went back downstairs and sat at his desk. He put the letter down carefully on the top of his desk and he took the check out of his pocket and placed it beside the letter. He had looked at them both at least a half dozen times, and nothing had changed. There it was in black and white in the letter: "Enclosed please find a check in the amount of $2,460.00," And there was the check, printed by the computer in black and white, certified by the First National Bank of Glenwood, signed with the personal signature of Clarence Greystone, President:

Greystone Spats Co.	December 12, 1997
Pay to the order of___James Duffy___	$246,000.00
___Two Hundred Forty Six Thousand___	DOLLARS
memo___severance pay___	*Clarence Greystone III* President
First National Bank of Glenwood	

Jim stared at the check and scratched his head. "Two hundred forty-six thousand instead of $2,460.00. Just a couple of decimal points," he mused. "It's obviously a computer mistake, but . . . Greystone signed it himself and the check is certified." And then as he thought about having devoted his whole life to the Greystone Spats Company he remembered the advice Greystone had given him. *"You see, that's always been your problem, Duffy. You don't have any vision. You worry about the small stuff, you have to think big for once in your life. THINK THE WAY I DO."*

"I'm going to try to do that, Mr. Greystone," Jim said aloud, as he picked up the phone.

"Gulliver's Travel."

"Yes, ma'am, this is Mr. Duffy again. I want to cancel my tickets to Daytona. Sorry I troubled you. Thank you very much." Jim hung up the phone and dialed once more.

"Jet-a-way Travel Agency, Gail speaking."

"I would like a couple of tickets to Brazil, please."

"Where exactly would you like to go in Brazil, sir?"

"Well, uh, ah, how about the capital?"

"Which one?"

"What do you mean, which one?"

"There are two capitals in Brazil, sir."

"I want to go to the biggest one," Jim replied.

"That would be Rio de Janeiro."

"That's exactly right, that's where I want to go," Jim said forcefully.

"When would that be, please?"

"Tomorrow, as soon as possible."

"Okay, let me just check and see what is available." Jim could hear the travel agent typing on her computer and muttering to herself as she checked out the options. Just as he was about to give up on her she said, "That's USAir leaving Buffalo at 2:35 P.M. to Miami, and Trans-Brazil departing Miami to Rio at 11:15 P.M. When is your date of return please?"

"Not sure," Jim said hesitantly. "How about two one-way tickets?

"We can do that for you. Is there anything else we can help you with?

"As a matter of fact there is. Could you please tell me if it's winter or summer in Brazil right now?"

Chapter Eleven

MICHAEL AND DOC PUT THE food away and washed the dishes while Beth was reading *Spatsco*. Then they took their coffee into Doc's den to continue their discussion about the merits and demerits of HMOs. When Beth finished the story she joined them and said, "I have a question for you, Michael."

"Shoot."

"I want to know if *Spatsco* is a true story."

"First things first. Did you like it?"

"It's not my favorite, but it raises a couple of interesting questions. By the way, I knew Greystone. We served on several committees together, you know, the Chamber Charity Ball and the Country Club spring party. I thought he was a pompous little—anyway I want to know how you found out what happened."

"I got the story initially from Fran Borofsky, who was Greystone's private secretary for years. One day she and I were talking during lunch at the Lonesome Cafe about the Greystone Company closing down, and then she told me this wild tale about a computer mistake. I didn't pay much attention to her until she mentioned Jim Duffy . . . that's not his real name of course. I remembered him calling and asking me how a certified check works. Before I started to write the story, I called Fran to see if she knew how big the computer mistake was, and she told me the amount to the penny because she was still working for Greystone when it was discovered. The poetic justice part of all this is that when Greystone tried to cash his own severance pay check, which was not certified, it bounced because Jim Duffy's check wiped out the account."

"There really is a God," Beth said.

"That's the other thing, sort of a double whammy. When Greystone tried to sell the building to get his "perk," as he called it, they discovered it was loaded with asbestos and the cost of cleaning it up was prohibitive. No one wanted to buy the building because it couldn't be occupied the way it was, and it would cost a bundle to tear it down and cart it away. The last I heard, the Village acquired it for back taxes and is planning to demolish it and make a park on the land."

"Bravo!" Beth cheered.

"Are you up to reading one more?" Michael asked her hesitantly.

"Why not? It's just like being at the hairdresser's, where I get caught up on all the local gossip. The main difference is that there's damn little romance in your stories, but at the hairdresser's. . . . Wow."

"Okay, I'll drop it off in a day or two on my way to the office. But, wait a minute, I just got a great idea."

"What's that?" Beth asked warily.

"Since it's my last story, I will be looking for new material. Maybe my next group of stories could all originate in Millie's Hair Salon. Every week after you visit her shop, you would pass along all the juiciest gossip to me."

"I could never do that!" Beth said, scowling.

"Why not, for goodness' sake?"

"Anything a woman hears at the beauty parlor is considered a privileged communication," she replied smugly.

"I don't believe you, Beth. First you tell me the beauty salon is the source of all the most scandalous rumors in the village, and now you're telling me that what you hear there is confidential?"

"Only as far as men are concerned," she replied haughtily. "Besides which, all the stories I hear there are unprintable."

"I could call the series 'Sex and a Rinse' or how about—"

Doc, who had been nodding off, suddenly perked up. "Did someone mention sex?"

"Go back to sleep, Doc," Michael said, "the concept is over your head."

"I agree with you, Mike," Beth nodded.

"How come you always take his side?" Doc whined.

"Because I'm not married to him, I suppose, but in this instance . . . "

"It's okay, Beth, I know he means well, he just happens to be illiterate."

"Listen, Buster, I read Ann Landers every day."

"That's true Mike. He does. Religiously. She is one of his idols."

"Now listen to me, guys, that lady has her act together," Doc said.

"He says that because she always advises people to check with their doctor if it's for a hangnail or hemorrhoids."

"Right on!" Doc pumped his fist in the air.

"Could we get back to discussing my story, please?" Michael pleaded.

"Look, Donald, why don't you read his story? It won't take you more than twenty minutes, and then we can all discuss it."

"Remember, Beth, he's a slow reader unless he's reading a thermometer. Make it half an hour."

"Okay, give me the damn story. But it better not have

anything to do with medical malpractice." Doc picked up the story and marched into his den. Later when Michael went in to check on how Doc was coming along with his story, he found him asleep with page three of *Spatsco* clenched in his hand.

Even though the references to sex were fleeting and innocuous, after Michael left Doc and Beth, his thoughts wandered in that direction as he drove along the lonely road toward his home. He glanced at the clock on the dash: 9:45. He decided that if he waited until he arrived home it would surely be too late to call. He pulled over to the side of the winding road and dialed information on his car phone. When he got the number he wanted, he dialed again.

"Hi Martha, Michael O'Leary. Could I speak with Lucette? "

"Sure, she's right here."

"Hi Michael."

"If you can remember as far back as last Saturday night, you suggested that a tramp through the woods might be fun, and I want to know whether you still think it's a good idea."

"Absolutely. My sisters and I are talked out and I am raring to get up and go."

"Well, I thought tomorrow we might pack a picnic basket, and like I said, we can hike up to the fire tower at the top of Hogback Mountain and see my friend Marc. I could call him and invite him to lunch in his own cabin. It gets pretty lonely up there, especially at this time of year."

"What a lovely idea. Do you trust me to make the lunch?"

"You read my mind. I'll bring the wine and carry everything up the mountain. Now I don't suppose you have your own snowshoes?"

"No, Counselor, and in fact I don't know one end of a snowshoe from the other. But I'm a quick learner."

"I am painfully aware of what a quick learner you are. It certainly didn't take you long to figure me out."

"Oh dear, I was hoping you had forgotten all about that conversation. I'm afraid I'm not what you call a shrinking violet. But as they say, when you get to know me. . . . "

"I will *never* forget it and I will never make such a terrible mistake again, ever. And as for getting to know you, that is the whole purpose of this adventure. How about I pick you up around 9:30 in the morning? I'll bring a pair of shoes for you. What do you like, red or white?"

"Shoes or wine?"

"You sound just like my best friend. He was the piano player at the party. I'd like you to meet him and his wife Beth, but I guess it's best to climb one mountain at a time."

"I'm looking forward to tomorrow," she said as she hung up the phone.

"I think it's going to be interesting," Michael said to himself.

It took them over two hours of tough going to reach Marc's cabin. Its location had been carefully selected to provide a 360 degree view of the forests below. Lucette described the day as a "zippity do da" day. During the climb Michael learned that she was an assistant professor of chemistry at Columbia University and was recovering from a painful divorce.

After a spectacular lunch, they sat comfortably in front of Marc's fire sipping their red wine. Although he had television and was up to date on all the news of the day, he was starved for human companionship. He told them stories about his life as a forest ranger that made them laugh and cry. He was ruggedly handsome and unpretentious, with a warm sense of humor. Lucette appeared to be fascinated by him, and Michael felt a twinge of jealousy as he appraised the situation.

They took their leave in time to complete the return trip before dark. Marc urged them to return whenever they could. By the look in Lucette's eyes Michael was convinced she would be returning soon. "I can't blame her a bit," he thought as they hiked silently back down the mountain. They spoke very little driving back to her sister's, and by the time he escorted her up to the front door he was totally depressed. He was about to struggle through an awkward farewell when she stepped close to him and said, "I do believe that it has been one of the loveliest days I can remember in such a long time. The weather was perfect, your friend Marc is an absolute delight, I am so physically exhausted that I will probably fall asleep before dinner. And you, Michael O'Leary, are a very nice man. Will you call me again?"

"Yes, of course," he stammered. "I mean how about dinner tomorrow night?"

"I would like that very much," she whispered. Then she kissed him lightly on the cheek and slipped inside. He felt as if he had just caught a pass in the end zone.

On his way home, he stopped at Doc's to invite them for dinner at his place the following night.

"Would you like a glass of eggnog?" Beth asked when he showed up in her kitchen.

"No thanks, I'm eggnogged out. Where's Doc?"

"Still at the hospital, but he should be along any minute. I'm exhausted from shopping and wrapping presents. I can't wait to give you yours."

"You're just saying that to make certain I don't forget you, right? By the way, how about you and Doc joining Lucette and me for dinner at my place tomorrow night?"

"Lucette who?" she asked casually.

"Oh, you know," he answered.

"No, I don't know or I wouldn't have asked. I never heard you speak of her before. Where is she from? Is this something serious? Why all the mystery? I don't understand you, Michael. Doc is supposed to be your best friend and you don't tell him anything."

"I tell him everything he ever asks me, but he never asks."

"Well, I do,"

"Okay, okay, Aunt Lucette is my mother's first cousin on her father's side."

"You're not funny, you know, Michael. Do you want me to tell you what I thought about your stories or do you want me to tell you what you can do with them first?"

"I think I'll wait a while for your comments, at least until after you meet Aunt Lucette."

They all arrived at Michael's place at exactly the same time, and walked up the front path together. Michael cooked steaks over a charcoal grill which was sitting in two feet of snow in the back yard, He wore his sheepskin coat, leather work gloves and a coonskin cap as he seasoned and grilled the two-inch-thick sirloins. By the time he brought the sizzling steaks to the table, Beth and Lucette were chatting away like old friends and the evening was off to a fine start. When the dishes were cleared away, they all gathered around the massive old fieldstone fireplace. Lucette appeared to be totally at ease.

"Lucette, did you know that in addition to being a

mediocre attorney, a fair tennis player, and a terrible pool player, my Irish friend here is also a short story writer whose talent is questionable?" Doc said.

"Thanks. I really needed that."

"You know I'm only kidding. In fact, I liked *Jack O' Hearts* a lot, Mike. I think it might be good enough for *The New Yorker*."

"Unfortunately, *The New Yorker* doesn't think so." Michael opened a drawer in his desk, removed a note and handed it to Doc.

THE
NEW YORKER
20 WEST 43RD STREET
NEW YORK, NY 10036-7441

(212) 840-3800

We regret that we are unable
to use the enclosed material.
Thank you for giving us the
opportunity to consider it.

The Editors

"So that's what a rejection slip looks like," Doc said. "It doesn't have your name on it, maybe they got it mixed up with someone else's story."

"Afraid not. They clipped their note right to the manuscript when they returned it."

"Well, as far as I'm concerned, they made a big mistake," Doc said, loyal to his friend.

Lucette turned to Michael, "What's the story about?" she asked.

"A toilet," Doc interjected with a chuckle.

"You wrote a story about a toilet?" Lucette laughed, wrinkling up her nose.

"Sort of," Michael smiled, "but I've just finished my last story. I know Doc will enjoy it because there is a doctor in it.

"Can I read it?" Lucette asked.

"Only if you have Christmas Eve dinner with me at Papagallos Restaurant," Michael responded.

"I don't care whether you accept Mike's dinner invitation at Papagallos, but you must join us for our traditional Christmas Day goose dinner," Beth urged. "We would love to have you. You have to bring three presents to put under the tree which can't cost more than five dollars each. Then we take turns opening the mystery packages, but the hooker is that if you don't like the present you open you can swap it for any other present that someone else has previously opened, and they have to give it to you. Last year Mike got stuck with two goldfish, a box of crayons and a size 44 DD-cup bra."

"I kept the goldfish and the crayons and offered the bra to Beth, but she claimed it was too small for her," Michael said.

"You are gross, O'Leary, and on that note we are leaving before you try to rope us into helping with the dishes," Beth pronounced.

Lucette and Michael worked together cleaning up the kitchen and then they took their coffee into the living room and lounged in front of the fire.

"What is the name of the story that I must read in order to earn my Christmas Eve dinner?" Lucette asked.

"It's called *Flesh of My Flesh.*" Michael retrieved the story from his desk and handed it to her. "Is it possible you could read it sometime tomorrow and then tell me what you think?"

"Believe it or not, my kid sister is a writer. Pretty good too. She makes me read everything before she sends it to her agent. I love doing it. It's fun. She claims I'm the only one who takes the job seriously, but we fight about her writing all the time. I don't think I want to fight with you, Michael," she said softly.

"Sometimes it takes a good rowdy fight to find the truth. That's how the judicial system works. Two professionals, toe to toe, slugging it out, and believe it or not, nine times out of ten the jury gets it right," Michael said earnestly.

"I don't know anything at all about the art of advocacy. John spent ten or twelve hours a day helping to put together mergers of large companies."

"I assume you are talking about your husband, John, and I'll bet he spent a good many hours engineering hostile takeovers as well."

"Yes, that's true, but to his credit, he hated it."

"If he hated it, why did he do it?"

"For money I suppose. Maybe that's why he's not my husband, he's my *former* husband. But can you say that you never do anything in your practice just for money?"

"How come you always seem to catch me with my philosophical pants down? Of course I do things sometimes just to pay the rent. I was being a pompous ass again," he countered, shaking his head and getting up to refill their glasses.

"I think you are being too hard on yourself," she said. "But why don't you tell me something you did recently just to pay the rent," she laughed holding up her glass.

"Good question. Let me think a minute," Michael said sitting down beside her on the sofa facing the fire and putting his feet up on the coffee table. "Okay, for example, a week ago a young woman came into my office and asked me how she could commit murder without having to go to jail for the rest of her life."

"You must be kidding."

"It's the truth, I swear. I charged her twenty-five dollars for reading the legal definition of murder to her."

"But that's terrible, Michael."

"I'd say it was on par with a hostile takeover. Besides, I think she was just curious, she didn't look like the type of person who would actually kill someone."

They sat silently for a few minutes, staring into the fire. Lucette broke the silence. "I want to say something Michael, but it is very important that you don't take it the wrong way. Promise?"

"It's dangerous to make a promise without having a clue as to what you are promising to do . . . or not to do," he said smiling. She took a sip of her drink and hesitated before speaking.

"What I want to say is . . . we have known each other for such a short time . . . " she turned her head away from the fire and looked directly into his eyes, "and . . . "

"And what?"

"And I have become very fond of you, Michael O'Leary." He pulled her close to him and they kissed tenderly.

"If I put on one of my favorite holiday records would you dance with me Professor Graham?"

"I thought you would never ask," she replied.

When Bing Crosby began to sing "I'm Dreaming of a White Christmas," he reached out to her and she slipped into his arms.

"Shall we dance the night away?" Lucette whispered, laying her head on his shoulder. "Would the heroine in any of your stories ever ask a question as corny as that, Michael?"

"Absolutely. Like Beth says, I'm a story teller, not a true writer." When the song ended, Lucette said, "I have had an absolutely enchanting evening, and I adore Doc and Beth. How lucky you are to have them as your best friends."

"It was terribly important to me that you would all like each other."

"I don't know how they feel about me, but I'm sold."

"Doc told me that he thinks you are the cat's pajamas, which I must tell you is his highest accolade, and Beth gave me the thumbs up sign once as you were leaving the room."

"The cat's pajamas. . . . What more could I ask?"

Since it had begun to storm again, Michael suggested to Lucette that she could spend the night if she wished, but she graciously declined his offer. Michael walked her out to her car and brushed several inches of snow off her windshield. He waited to make certain her car would start. The engine coughed a few times but finally took hold. Lucette rolled her window down. Michael leaned in through the window and gave her a brief good night kiss. He didn't want her to leave.

"I promise I will read *Flesh of My Flesh* right after I finish my first cup of coffee tomorrow morning. When shall I call you to talk about it?"

"I'm going to wait right at home until I hear from you. Remember now, I'm thick-skinned so I expect you to tell me exactly what you think."

"You must know by now I don't have a problem with that."

"Ouch! Okay, so as long as you tell me it is an absolutely marvelous story on a par with *Romeo and Juliet* we are going to continue to get along just fine."

"Good night, Shakespeare," she said, stepping on the gas and driving recklessly down the driveway. Michael stared after her until she turned onto the main road and out of sight, then he trudged back to his empty house. He settled into his favorite chair trying to decide whether to go to bed or put another log on the fire. He studied the dying embers and began to think about the woman who had just left his embrace.

"What is there about her that is different from all the others?" he wondered aloud as he got up from his chair and went over to his desk. He picked up a yellow legal pad and returned to his place in front of the fire. He drew a vertical line down the center of the page labeling the left column "Assets" and the right column "Liabilities." In the left hand column he wrote: "attractive, intelligent, sense of humor, integrity, Doc and Beth approve."

In the right column he made a single comment. "Not likely to consider moving to Glenwood without a long-term commitment."

He awakened earlier than usual the next morning. After he showered and shaved, it was still only 7:15. His thoughts had immediately returned to Lucette. "I think I'm hooked," he said to his dog Kodiak as he started to cook breakfast. "The problem is I don't really know her. And we're not in a position to pursue this affair in the traditional way. Do you understand that, Kody?" The dog, a mixture of Huskie and German Shepherd, wagged his tail vigorously, sensing that something unusual was in the making. "You see, if she lived close by, we could get to know each other over a period of time. But the way it is, if things don't heat up before she goes back to New York, we will each get caught up in our regular routines, which won't leave room for skipping down the yellow brick road together. What do you think, Kody?" The dog barked and put his paw up on Michael's lap. "With a friend like you, who needs a woman anyway, right?"

Kody barked again.

Lucette poured herself a second cup of coffee and went back up to her bedroom to read Michael's story. She was less interested in the story than she was in learning something more about its author. Her feelings for him had escalated dramatically during the previous evening, but she recognized that she was vulnerable. Her marriage had been in shambles for several years and Michael was the first man she had met since her divorce.

"I've only known him a few days. What am I thinking of?" she asked herself. "The ink isn't dry on my hard-earned, emotionally devastating, very expensive divorce decree and . . . what about his feelings for me? I told him, in schoolgirl fashion, that I was fond of him, and his only response was to invite me to spend the night with him. When I turned him down, he didn't try to persuade me otherwise, all he did was shrug his shoulders and ask me to call him first thing in the morning and tell him what I thought of his damned short story."

She laughed at herself and climbed back into bed with the story in hand.

Chapter Twelve

Flesh of My Flesh

We were just two immature college kids. We didn't realize how much effort it took to make a marriage work. I knew we were in trouble when my wife caught the seven-year itch at the end of seven months of marriage. I was divorced at age twenty-two. Whenever anyone asked, "When are you going to get married again?" my stock answer was, "Why would I want to stick beans up my nose twice?"

I received my masters degree in architecture and went to work for Massey & Fox, a highly respected firm with offices in several major cities in the U.S. I was assigned to work in Rochester, New York, where I began my climb up the professional ladder. The practice of architecture is an exciting mixture of art, science and business. Keeping these three elements in perspective is a most demanding task. Over the years I found very few of my colleagues capable of preventing the demands of the marketplace from dominating the practice, but I was quite good at convincing our clients that good design and business objectives were not incompatible. I spent most of my waking hours at the drafting table during my first five years with the firm, but then I got lucky. The president of one of our corporate clients was impressed with some sketches I made for a new industrial park they were going to build just outside Phoenix and I was selected to supervise the job there.

I found an old adobe cabin built on the side of Camelback Mountain in Scottsdale and settled in for the duration. Although I didn't have a lot of time for socializing, I managed to play some tennis and did my fair share of boozin' and beddin' on the weekends. I got some pretty good press for my design of the buildings, which brought in enough work to warrant my staying in Arizona through the sixties. I spent a little over ten years working in the Southwest and enjoyed every moment of it. I would probably have spent the rest of my life there, but the day after my fortieth birthday I was made a partner in the firm and ordered back east to take over the management of the Rochester office. I hesitated before accepting the offer to return to the Northeast, because I had come to love the people, the climate and the lifestyle around Phoenix, but the firm upped the ante and announced that I would be chief designer of a multimillion dollar residential and commercial community on Lake Ontario. The professional and financial rewards they offered me were enough to bring me back to snow country, and I packed my bags.

On the flight back to New York I met Kerry. She was tall, upbeat, loved to dance and sail and hike and play tennis; she was a pro in the art of having fun. She lived in Dallas and worked for American Airlines as a flight attendant, although in those days she was called a hostess. For six months we chased each other all over the country. It was an expensive but exhilarating affair with several short trips to Mexico and the Caribbean thrown in for good measure. There was no opportunity for quiet time because we were racing at breakneck speed to satisfy every hedonistic whim that entered our minds.

One night when we were visiting Matt and Ginny Winston, friends of hers who had a summer place on the Cape, we got into a discussion about *Brown vs. The Board of Education*, the Supreme Court decision which desegregated the schools in the South. I was particularly interested in the subject because I was born in the South and didn't come north until I went to college. In the middle of the discussion Kerry got up, turned her back on us, and peeled off all her clothes. Her beautiful body was tanned to perfection except for the tiny white patch on her rear. "I'm Brown and Bored with Education. It's skinny dipping time," she yelled as she ran down to the beach and plunged into the sea.

"Kerry sure knows how to put things in perspective," Matt chuckled, as we all jumped into our birthday suits and raced down to join her.

Two weeks later as I was driving down from Rochester to meet Kerry for a thrill-filled weekend in the Big Apple, the idea of marriage kept lurking in the deep recesses of my mind. I had clearly found the perfect woman after so many years of bachelorhood. Vietnam was a continuing stench that was tearing the country apart and Lyndon Johnson didn't know what the hell to do about it. I had turned forty-one and decided it was time to get off the Kerry-go-round. She and I had agreed to meet in New York for dinner, theater, listening and dancing at the Village Vanguard. I had booked a suite at the Park Lane Hotel overlooking Central Park, to boot.

We walked into Smith & Wollensky's Steakhouse on Third Avenue for drinks and an early meal before heading to the theater. The place was crowded with out-of-town executives on expense accounts, whooping it up everywhere. It was so packed we had to walk the gauntlet past the long bar in order to reach the table I had reserved. There must have been thirty guys jammed around the bar as we walked by, and to a man they stopped what they were saying to appraise Kerry with envy. She was wearing a white silk flimsy something or other held up by spaghetti straps, one of which she allowed to slip and remain off the shoulder nearest the bar. She turned her head toward me and smiled as we walked by, causing her shoulder-length ash blond hair to swirl about her face just the way they do it in the Clairol commercials. Her dangling silver and jade earrings sent sparks of color in every direction. I held her arm possessively as I guided her into the dining room, enjoying the attention she was getting with every step she took. If she had said, "I will not move another inch unless you marry me right now," I would have called for a justice of the peace to perform the ceremony on the spot. She was absolutely ravishing . . . she knew it . . . I knew it . . . everyone in the room knew it.

"Let's celebrate," she exclaimed, as we reached our table and settled in.

"What are we celebrating?" I asked, taking her hands in mine and whispering a kiss along her fingertips.

"I don't know . . . us . . . life . . . our anniversary . . . it's six months to the day . . . " she glanced at her watch, "almost to the hour when we met." She flashed me a smile that lit up the restaurant.

"That's good enough for me," I countered, making the decision then and there to pop the question when the champagne arrived. I raised my arm and signaled for a waiter. The staff was so busy I couldn't catch anyone's eye. A waiter finally arrived at our table and assured me that he would send the wine steward over to us immediately. Another ten minutes passed without anyone showing up. Kerry was furious. I was frustrated. We stopped talking. She lit a cigarette ostentatiously, took a few drags, stamped it out in the ashtray angrily and immediately lit another. Five more minutes passed. Her Miss America smile had disappeared.

"Let's go," she said, putting her cigarettes and lighter in her purse and checking her makeup. I reached over to calm her down, placing my hand gently on her arm.

"Just be patient, darling. I'm sure they will get to us as soon as they can. You can see the place is wild . . . we're lucky to have a table."

"Big deal. . . . It's the damn war." She said shrugging my hand off her arm.

"What the hell has the war got to do with not being able to get a drink?" I said laughing. She stared straight at me, her eyes blazing.

"Sometimes you are so stupid" she hissed. "If our boys weren't fighting in Vietnam, they would be back here doing what they are supposed to."

"You mean like waiting on our table . . . I don't believe you," I said, chuckling.

"That's exactly what I mean . . . instead of these jungle bunnies, we would have some decent waiters."

"Now wait a minute kiddo, that is a vicious, racist remark, and I . . . "

"You want to end this goddamn war . . . I'll tell you how . . . drop an atomic bomb on those freakin' gooks and that'll do it . . . that's what my daddy says and he's right."

I looked at her beautiful face . . . ugly now with malice. I realized for the first time that I had spent hours exploring every hidden inch of her body, but I hadn't devoted five minutes to discover what was going on in her screwed-up head.

I reached into my pocket for the two front row tickets to *Grease* and dropped them on the table.

"If you call right away, maybe your daddy can pick you up in time to see the show," I said. Then I turned and walked away. I never saw her again.

With two colossal failures under my belt I decided that I was just not programmed for long-term relationships and in the years that followed I dedicated myself to my work as I moved up to a position of leadership in the firm. I enjoyed many transient female friendships during that time, but I took a detour whenever anyone suggested a more permanent arrangement.

Around 1979 or 1980 we were awarded a contract to design a major urban commercial complex. My professional responsibilities became so demanding I didn't have time to consider that "life" might be passing me by. Nevertheless, when I was invited to dinner at the homes of friends and colleagues, to be matched up with single females in order to balance the chairs at the dinner table,

I often thought about the comfort and companionship that is supposed to accompany marriage, and I would wonder if I weren't missing out on something. Such thoughts were invariably dispelled with the advent of another agonizing divorce among my circle of friends, and I would happily return to my bachelor quarters.

I can't remember exactly when Maria Alvarez came to work for us as a graphic artist. She had just graduated from Bennington College with an impressive portfolio. Her job was to create renderings for the prospective tenants in our new project. She was a bright funny kid and conscientious as hell. She was charming, provocative and very pleasing to the eye. I caught myself thinking about her in a non-professional way sometimes when we worked together late into the night. I remember wishing that she weren't so young or I weren't so old.

On St. Patrick's Day I had invited everyone who was working on the job to have a green beer or two on me at Hooligan's Bar and Grill around the corner from our office. After consuming a pitcher of beer with a couple of complimentary shots of Irish whiskey all by myself as the only certifiable Irishman in the group, I was persuaded to sing a solo of "Danny Boy." I was rewarded with thunderous applause, but it's hard not to love a happy Irish drunk on St. Patrick's Day. I didn't want the party to end, but one by one my guests gave their thanks for the drinks and drifted off to hearth and home, leaving Maria and me to close down the bar. I had laughed too much, drunk too much, and eaten too little. I dozed off for a few minutes, and when I awakened I discovered that Maria was holding my hands in both of hers. She was looking into my eyes. I was totally embarrassed and started to ease my hands away. She resisted.

"Why are you avoiding me?" she asked, with a pained expression on her face.

"I have never avoided you, I mean, we think you are a wonderful kid and we are all delighted to have you with us." I stammered.

"First of all, I'm not a kid, I'm almost twenty-three years old. And secondly, I'm not talking professionally here, I'm talking about me, Maria Alvarez, five-foot-six, shoulder-length black hair, spectacular deep brown eyes, 36-24-34 and pretty good lookin' besides."

"But I . . . "

"Don't deny it Mr. McShane . . . see, you haven't even asked me to call you Paul. Everyone in the office calls you Paul except me."

"Well for God's sake, Maria, I don't know why . . . I mean I never . . . "

"What's wrong with me? Aren't you at least a little attracted to me? All the married guys in the office are hitting on me every day, and there you are, the only single male at Massey & Fox and you treat me like I don't exist."

"I've done no such thing," I said defensively. "You are a very attractive young woman almost thirty years younger than me as a matter of fact, and you are an employee. I am your boss, for God's sake, and besides. . ."

"Bull—I don't want to hear any more. I want you to take me home," she said standing up a little unsteadily.

"Of course I'll drive you home," I said, helping her put on her coat. The dialogue had my fuzzy mind racing.

She put her arm in mine and leaned her head on my shoulder as we walked slowly to the lot where my car was parked. Neither of us spoke from the time we left the bar until I pulled up in front of her apartment which was located in an old three-story brownstone on East Avenue. I walked around and opened the car door. A snowstorm had just begun, with big fluffy flakes drifting down around us. When she got out, she reached up with both hands and turned up my coat collar. She tilted her head back, smiled and said softly, "Would you like to come up for a bit?"

I took her hands down from my shoulders. "Maria, I don't think that's such a good idea. I'm not sure you understand what's going on here . . . maybe a little too much Irish whiskey. I'm old but I'm not disabled you know."

"I am very much aware of what you are. And I'm not drunk," she replied haughtily. "I was only suggesting that you might like a cup of coffee and some scrambled eggs and bacon."

My conscience warned me to decline the invitation, but the rest of me voted to accept. We walked up the three flights of stairs to her apartment tucked under the steep pitched roof of the old mansion. Except for a tiny kitchenette and bath, her living quarters consisted of one large room dominated by the largest four-poster bed I had ever seen. The dark hardwood floor was covered with hand-woven Mexican throw rugs and multicolored pillows of all sizes, shapes and textures. The walls were covered with her own recreations of paintings from Rubens to Picasso, except that although they were immediately recognizable, she had converted all of them into erotic drawings, expressing her own wild imagination. An overhead fan turned lazily, causing polished pieces of driftwood suspended from the ceiling to move sensually. She immediately lit candles that sent shadows cascading around the walls. When she flicked a switch I was surrounded by the sound of primitive drums and a solo saxophone. It was pretty obvious that I was not the first male to be invited to her living quarters. The room screamed sex!

"Do you like it?" she demanded, and without waiting for an answer, she laughed, "I knew you would." She clapped her hands.

"And how about this?" she exclaimed, pulling aside the netting surrounding the massive four-poster bed to reveal a huge smoked-glass mirror suspended above it.

"I need a drink," I said, sinking down into a "poof" chair that looked like a giant marshmallow topped with whipped cream.

"In a moment, señor," she said, shrugging her shoulders and letting her dress slide to the floor.

"Jesus, Maria," I groaned, trying to extricate myself from the pillow chair. Her eyes were on fire as she slipped into my arms.

After that night we became very cozy, which raised a few eyebrows at the shop, but I didn't give a cat's whisker. With the difference in our ages, it was difficult for me to believe that we could find pleasure with each other for very long outside the bedroom, but we did. She even shared my view that anything resembling a long-term commitment would probably be destructive of our growing friendship. She was crazy and wonderful. She taught me how to live "young" and I taught her how to live "wise." We were open to each other's ideas and dreams, and we spent many evenings cooking dinner together, reading, listening to music, catching a late night movie and falling asleep on the couch in a tangle of arms and legs.

After we had been hanging out for about two months, she approached me one day at work. She seemed sad. She asked if I could come to her place around seven. I said, "Sure, do you want me to pick up some Chinese?" She said that would be fine, but her eyes were dead. I couldn't figure it. Bids were due in on the contract for the office tower and we were all frantic preparing for the bid opening. I almost forgot our date, but managed to get there with the carry-out only a half-hour late. She was wearing one of those loose-fitting dresses that appear to be made out of burlap that the young women seem to adore. She kissed me perfunctorily and took the bottle of Chardonnay I had brought. She smiled, a little sadly I thought, but looked as delicious as ever despite the Omar the Tent-maker outfit she was wearing. She made me a drink and led me over to the marshmallow chair, and sat cross-legged at my feet. I knew something was up, but I didn't have a clue unless she was going to hand-deliver a "Dear John" letter to me. I took a sip of my drink and looked at her intently. She gazed up at me, wide-eyed. She seemed out of sync somehow.

"Well, here we are, Dear," she said. She had never called me "dear" before. Then she blurted it out, "I'm pregnant!" She began to giggle hysterically, and the next thing I knew she was bawling her eyes out. I took her in my arms and held her tight until she stopped sobbing. She stood up, paced back and forth a few steps and said, "We've got to talk, Honey." She had never called me "honey" before, either. I just couldn't figure it.

"I don't know what to do," she wailed, and began to cry all over again. I couldn't fathom what she was so upset about. She was "pro-choice," after all. She went into the bathroom. I waited. When she finally returned she looked at me fiercely and blurted it out. "Well . . . do you want the baby or not?" I was stunned! It just hadn't occurred to me that this had anything to do with me. I mean I figured it was her choice. Jesus, a baby!

"I'm fifty-two years old, Maria, I mean . . ."

"You're fifty-one!"

"I'm fifty-three as a matter of fact . . . I lied to you a little."

"Oh, God!" she started to whimper again. "I want to have the baby . . . but I'm scared and I need support and . . ."

"If it's money. . ." I said.

"It's not money!" she cried. "Well, it is money, but that's only part of it. I need someone to care about the baby and me . . . and . . . and . . . share it all with me."

"If you are asking me if I will share in the financial responsibility of caring for the child? . . . of course I will. It took two to tango. If you are asking me to share in the decision of whether or not you should have an abortion, I can tell you unequivocally . . . that is your decision alone. However, if you are asking me if I will share the responsibility of raising the baby, the answer is, *I don't think so.* I'm not ready to spend the balance of my life changing diapers and all the rest of it. Think about it, Maria, when the kid graduates from high school, I will be over seventy years old. I'm afraid it's just not for me."

"How can you say that?" she hissed. "He's half yours!"

"Okay, you have my permission to abort my half." I replied thoughtlessly.

"You bastard!" she cried, coming after me with both fists swinging. I grabbed her arms and held her close to me until she calmed down. After a long silence, she laid her head on my shoulder and sobbed, "Why can't you see that it is your problem too?" I hesitated a long time before answering her.

"Look, Maria, you must understand that twenty minutes ago I didn't know I had a problem. On the other hand, you must have been living with the idea of having a baby for a month or so. In retrospect, I should have made certain that you were on the pill or whatever that first time. I just took it for granted that when a twenty-two-year-old woman invites a man to bed without any . . . ah . . . discussion about precautions . . . it means that she has protected herself. Obviously I was mistaken about that, and I am prepared to pay the financial price for that mistake, whatever your decision may be. But if you choose to have the baby, I don't think it is fair to ask me to spend the rest of my life being tied down to the day-to-day mechanics of raising a child."

"Mechanics? Is that what you think having a child is . . . mechanics?"

"Call it whatever you wish, but I can assure you that for the next five years of your life, you will be dealing with the distasteful but absolutely necessary mechanical tasks of wiping snotty noses and shitty asses."

"You make it sound so horrible, and it's not!" she said, stamping her foot.

"You've never done it," I challenged.

"Neither have you!"

We argued for hours, finished off one bottle of wine and started on another. She became more rational and I became more sensitive to the situation. At some time around two o'clock in the morning, we reached an agreement. She was going to have the baby and I was going to help her financially and in whatever other way I could without abandoning my own plans for the future. It was a silly, unworkable compromise but it seemed to satisfy both of us at the time and we fell asleep in each other's arms.

During the balance of her pregnancy we remained friends and lovers. I don't know exactly whose idea it was, but in the beginning of her seventh month, we decided to get married in order to legitimize the child. He or she would be called Patrick or Patricia in honor of the Saint who had blessed his/her conception. We were married in city hall and then informed our parents that we had been secretly married for a year and were about to have our first-born. My seventy-five-year-old mother was ecstatic. It would be her only grand-child. But Maria's parents, who lived in Puerto Rico where she was born, were apprehensive. They had never met me, and they were not at all fooled by the secret marriage nonsense. They were very upset that they had not been given the opportunity to appraise and approve the groom. We promised to visit them immediately, and we did.

I had been to Puerto Rico once for a long weekend, but my time there had been spent lounging around the pool, fooling around in the room, dressing up for a fancy dinner and gam-bling until the wee hours of the morning. I had never left my high-rise hotel until the taxi took me back to the airport.

Maria and her family, on the other hand, introduced me to the heart and soul of Puerto Rico . . . the music, the dancing, the laughter and the meaning of "family" Puerto Rican style. When we weren't singing or dancing we were eating and drinking. Everyone worked hard all day and played hard all night. I was very self-conscious about my age, especially when Maria introduced me to all her friends who were her own age, but it didn't seem to bother anyone except me. I quickly learned that old men marrying young girls was commonplace in Puerto Rico, and when I met Maria's uncle Juan Carlo, I became convinced. He was seventy-three years old and had a twenty-five-year-old wife and a three-year-old daughter who was a year younger than his latest grandchild. He and his wife threw a big party for us at their summer home in Humacao. It was situated overlooking the sea on the northwest coast of Puerto Rico. It took us two hours to drive there from San Juan.

I hadn't realized how big and spectacularly beautiful the island really was. Nor did I know how wonderfully warm and gentle the people of Puerto Rico were once you traveled twenty miles outside San Juan. I had always considered San Juan and Puerto Rico to be synonymous, but I was badly mistaken about that. Maria pointed out to me that I would be very upset if the people of the world judged America by the mean streets of Los Angeles or Miami. Maria's mother claimed that everyone on the island knew that,

with the exception of her daughter, all the unsa-
vory Puerto Ricans had been exiled to New York
City. Although she laughed when she said it, I
think she really believed it. After I had met,
kissed and danced with every aunt, niece and
female cousin, and consumed gallons of rum
with all the male relatives, we flew home to face
the world according to Patrick or Patricia.

Patrick surprised us by showing up early
on December 3, 1981. He was the ugliest baby I
had ever seen. Since I hadn't seen any other one-
day-old babies before, it was an unnerving experience. He had spiky jet-black hair, his nose
seemed to be askew and he was wrinkled like an
old man. I was certain that I was responsible for
the wrinkles. On the other hand, he had very
respectable-sized testicles which I took credit for.
The nurses all said he was beautiful, but of course
they say that to all the new fathers. Maria seemed
very pleased with him. She kept counting fingers and toes and scrutinizing his ears and his
private parts to make sure everything was where
it was supposed to be. His vocal chords were
certainly where they were supposed to be.

I guess it happened the first time the nurse
put him in my arms and showed me how to hold
up his head so it wouldn't fall off. I expected

him to start bawling, but he didn't. He just sort of looked me straight in the eye, and I thought he smiled at me but everyone said he was too young to do that. I was hooked! I couldn't believe it. All my preconceptions went out the window when that kid was born. Patrick Juan Alvarez McShane brought me into the fold. I became a believer.

On his first birthday the three of us had a party. I gave him a baseball autographed by Roberto Clemente. Out of the blue, Maria said, "I made an appointment to see a lawyer tomorrow."

"You mean about making out our wills? Do I look sick or something?" I chided.

"No, but the year is up. In fact, my dear, it was up two months ago."

"What are you talking about?"

"Our agreement . . . the divorce . . . remember? We were only supposed to be married for a year. You were planning to get on with your own life after one year of marriage."

"Don't be ridiculous. Everything has changed since then."

"Oh?" she said with raised eyebrows. "I don't remember discussing any changes."

"There was no reason to discuss it. Hasn't it been obvious in the way I have cared for

Patrick? He's my son. I love him . . . I love you. I thought you understood all that," I said, beginning to panic.

"What about your *lifestyle* and your plans for the future that interfered with becoming a father? That's what prompted the agreement in the first place. 'Hedging your bets,' I believe you called it."

"What are you getting at, Maria?" I demanded, warily.

"I just want to know what my role is now, today. Am I married until death do us part, or am I a lover, standby wife and mother, waiting for the other shoe to drop?"

"I guess I never thought of that," I said sheepishly. "I should have, I suppose, but I assumed you knew that after I became a father my plans for the future changed."

"Do I take that to mean you like being a father?" she asked cautiously.

"What do you think?" I replied, picking Patrick up in my arms possessively.

"I'm pleased to hear that, darling," she said, with a sort of goofy grin, "because . . . you're going to be a father again."

"Are you serious?" I asked foolishly, knowing very well she wouldn't joke about such a thing. "Maybe I better negotiate a new contract," I teased, opening my arms wide to hold both of them close to me.

Margaret Maria McShane was born six months later, three days before my fifty-fourth birthday.

Maria went back to the drawing board as soon as "Maggie" entered kindergarten, but she didn't return to my firm. We both felt strongly that spending twenty-four hours a day together would be begging for trouble.

Although the passion between us dwindled, we settled into a traditional family unit, except that I took a more active role as a parent than most fathers, especially after Maria returned to work. Her new job allowed her to be much more creative, but it was very demanding. With the kids and our professional responsibilities, our time together and our social life slowed to a crawl. The Monday-to-Friday routine consisted of getting the kids off to school, work, dinner, spending some time with them before their bedtime, some reading in bed and then blessed sleep. There were a few variations, but not many. The weekends were equally routine. Saturday morning we worked around the house. Saturday afternoon there was little league baseball in the summer, small fry football in the fall and pee wee hockey in the winter for Patrick, who had the makings of a first-class athlete. I managed to watch him play in almost every game. I was always the oldest father in attendance and on more than one occasion was mistaken for his grandfather. He and I spent many hours hanging out together, watching ball games, fishing, sailing and camping. I could tell Maggie was also going to be a fine athlete, but she was not consumed by it the way Patrick was. She also showed interest in music, but at that age you really couldn't tell what the future held.

Maria was a spectacular mother, giving the kids whatever time they needed with her, but at the same time, teaching them to be independent, respectful, and responsible.

Maria and I reserved Sunday mornings for our individual pursuits which meant aerobics for her and tennis for me. Sunday afternoons were free, and I usually ended up watching a ball game on television through the winter and working around the house and garden in the summer. Occasionally we visited friends, but as the years slipped by, I became less willing to leave our home to go out and socialize.

Looking back on it I can see that things began to change in the summer of '91 when

Maria took a new job working for a company that produced television commercials. The people in her new office were young and mostly single . . . talented, slightly off-the-wall by my standards, carefree . . . into pot and stronger stuff, I suspected.

I'm pretty sure that was the year Maria wanted us to join a neighborhood dance club but I told her that my dancing days were over. I used to love to dance, and remembered dancing with Kerry until dawn on many occasions, but the music had changed since then, and now I considered it hard work with no reward. She nagged at me until I agreed to take her to a new disco club that had opened which featured her favorite Salsa and Calypso music. When we arrived, the place was jammed with pot smoking kids. It was so loud it was impossible to talk, and when she dragged me onto the dance floor, we were bumped and pushed and stomped upon from all directions. After a torturous hour when I was ready to call it quits, Maria's friends were just arriving. Finally when I could no longer keep my eyes open despite the volume of the music, I told her I was leaving with or without her. She begged me to stay a little longer so she could have a few dances with her friends, but I was tired and bored and suggested she get a lift home with Linda, one of her co-workers.

She was up bright and early the next morning in a happy mood. She thanked me for letting her hang out with her friends after I left. She didn't mention the time she got home, and I didn't ask.

Next came the "sailing" venture. Maria had met a young couple down the block who had a sailboat on Lake Ontario. They invited us to go sailing with them one weekend. I really didn't want to go, but it seemed that lately I had been saying no to all the things she wanted to do . . . skiing in Aspen . . . attending a rock concert with the "Who" or the "What" or some other far-out group of imbeciles with painted faces and bare chests and presumably no eardrums. So I agreed to go sailing. It was a disaster. The "sailboat" was a little twelve-foot cat boat that could barely hold the four of us. I had sailed all my life, but the kid who owned the boat didn't really know how to sail. It was a scorching day with very little wind and they had forgotten to put anything to drink on board. The three of them spent most of the time swimming around the boat, laughing and having a wonderful time. I hadn't brought any swimming trunks because I understood we were going sailing, not swimming, but even if I had, I'm sure I wouldn't have been able to climb back into the boat. I tried to teach the kid a bit about sailing, but he seemed to be more interested in horsing around in the water with Maria, so I gave up.

She joined our community theater that fall and became a local celebrity. Taking over all responsibility for artistic direction, which included costumes and set designs, she put her creative skills to work with spectacular results. I can't really say the family suffered from her new obsession with the theater, because although she spent less time at home, it was obvious that she was deriving tremendous pleasure from her work with the theater, and her happiness was reflected in the way she responded to each of us. The director, Larkin Steiner, was a very talented young man, and between them they set Rochester's theater enthusiasts on their ears. But it was their production of *Phantom of the Opera*, in collaboration with the Eastman School of Music and the Rochester Philharmonic that gained national acclaim. A vice president of an independent film company happened to be in town on the night *Phantom* opened. From the moment the curtain rose on the first act, he said afterward, he was overwhelmed by the high quality of the whole production, especially the set designs. When the final curtain fell to thunderous applause and the players returned for a dozen curtain calls, Mr. Hollywood went backstage to meet the cast and crew. He was invited to the cast party, and before he left he had offered Maria a job with his company. He had also talked at length to Larkin Steiner, but it was only Maria who received a concrete proposal. She was thrilled by the offer but quickly advised him that she was a wife and mother and although it sounded exciting beyond her wildest dreams, it was incompatible with her family commitments. He said he understood, but that he would be in touch with her after he returned to the west coast and she had had an opportunity to think about it. She was earning $45,000 at the company where she worked; Mr. Hollywood offered her $75,000.

She was on a high that continued into the spring of the following year. We had somehow gotten past the rough spots with the disco and sailing disasters. With our whirlwind separate professional lives and trying to keep up with the kids, we didn't have a lot of time to spend together, but after Maria got involved in the theater, things seemed better between us than they had been in years. On my sixty-fifth birthday we went out to dinner at the John Thomas Steakhouse. We had the "Porterhouse for Two," garlic mashed potatoes, sautéed wild mushrooms, and green salad, and we consumed two bottles of Dom Perignon in the process. After all, sixty-five is a big one, especially when your wife is only thirty-four. Maria seemed preoccupied throughout the meal and there were many long gaps in the conversation. When I reminisced about the St. Patrick's Day party that had started it all eleven years earlier, she began to cry, but I couldn't tell if she was sad or just sentimental. The second bottle of Champagne seemed to help lighten the mood and when I suggested that we drive over to the lake and park in our favorite spot, she didn't resist. We ended up making love that night for the first time in many months. I figured we were back on track, and the next morning's hangover was a small price to pay.

But then came what I shall always remember as "Black Friday." It was only a few days after my birthday. I had cooked dinner and we were all waiting for Maria to come home so we could eat together. She was often late from work on Fridays, so I didn't pay much attention to it except I was pissed because the roast was going to be overdone. When she didn't show up by nine o'clock, we ate dinner without her. It was after ten when she called.

"Hi, sorry I couldn't make it for dinner."

"That's okay," I lied. I was relieved to hear her voice. "I can pop the roast into the microwave when you get home."

"Well the thing is, I'm going out to dinner with the gang. We finished the McAllister job just under the wire and the old man is really pleased. We're going to grab a bite at this new club. It will probably be a late night."

"Okay, it sounds like fun. You deserve a night out on the town," I replied, with more enthusiasm than I felt.

"Thanks," she said, and hung up. I waited up for her for a while, but finally I fell asleep watching the late night movie.

I was awakened by the phone at 3:15 in the morning.

"Paul."

"Where the hell are you?"

"We're at the Sorensen Hotel, and I'm going to stay over. I've had too much to drink and I shouldn't drive."

"I'll come get you. Where's the hotel?" I demanded.

"No s'alright. We're jus' havin' some fun, everything's okay." She hung up. I immediately looked in the yellow pages under "Hotels and Motels" but there wasn't any Sorensen Hotel in the book. Nor anything that came close to it. I called information. No such hotel was listed. I went wild! I had no idea where to begin to look for her. I stayed up all night. When the kids got up late the next morning, I made breakfast for them and then took them to the mall and gave them enough money to buy new Reeboks and see a double header at the cinema.

Maria pulled in at 1:30 in the afternoon looking like hell. Her eyes were red from booze or crying or both. She went straight through to the bathroom and locked the door. I had started drinking myself, and without sleep I wasn't in the best of shape. I pounded on the bathroom door.

"Where the fuck have you been?" I demanded. She didn't answer. I yelled at her a few more times, poured myself another double whiskey and settled down to wait for her to come out.

She stayed in the john for more than an hour. When she came out I was still steaming. She looked better, but I could tell from the way she held her head that we were in for a fight.

"So where the hell were you?" I snarled

"I'm taking the kids and going to California with Larkin," she said defiantly.

"Like hell you are," I said, raising my fist in the air and taking a step toward her.

She covered her face with her arms and stood her ground. I grabbed the nearest table lamp and threw it against the wall. It hit the big gilt frame mirror which also came crashing to the floor. She ran upstairs and locked herself in the bedroom. I pounded on the door.

"Leave me alone," she cried. I ran into Patrick's room which was right next to ours and picked up a baseball bat. I started to smash in the bedroom door. She called the police and locked herself in the master bathroom. I threw the bat away and went downstairs and had another whiskey. I knew I was getting pretty drunk, but I didn't give a cat's ass. Two cops showed up with their siren wailing. There was a white guy and a big black guy. I told them they weren't needed, but they demanded to speak with Maria. They made note of the smashed lamp and the broken glass from the mirror all over the floor. They went upstairs and found Maria and the splintered bedroom door. They escorted her back down to the living room. I leaned against the wall, sullen, drinking and watching while they took a written statement from her. Everything she said was true. She didn't exaggerate anything. She didn't have to. She said she wanted an order of protection. When the black cop suggested that I lay off the booze, I said, "Go fuck yourself, you can't stop me from drinkin' in my own house." He shrugged his shoulders.

After Maria signed her affidavit, the white son of a bitch got up and came over to me. He put his hand on my arm. I pushed him away. Within a couple of seconds they had me on the floor with my hands cuffed behind my back, but I managed to slug the white guy in the side of the head on my way down. It seemed to me at the time that they had no right to do what they were doing. This was a matter between my wife and me in the privacy of my own home, for Christ's sake.

"Okay, McShane," the black cop said, "just so's there's no misunderstanding here, you're under arrest." Then he read me my rights from a card he pulled out of his wallet.

"You guys must be crazy. What the hell did I do except break up a little furniture in my own house? I never touched my wife."

"For now," the cop said, "the charges are

attempted assault with a deadly weapon against the person of Maria Alvarez-McShane, resisting arrest and assaulting an officer. The district attorney will probably have a few more ideas."

The white guy said, "Okay, pops, let's go," and then they dragged me down the sidewalk to the squad car. As they started to push me into the back seat, my kids showed up. Patrick saw me and ran up to the car.

"Hey, what are you doing, that's my—" he started to push the cop out of the way to get to me.

"Easy does it, boy," the white guy said, gripping him by the shoulder. "We're just taking Gramps here for a little ride down to the station."

"What did you do, Daddy?" Maggie cried, tears streaming down her cheeks. Maria came out and gathered up the kids as we drove away.

The grand jury indicted me on three felony counts. My $10,000 criminal lawyer negotiated a deal with the D.A. and within a week of my arrest I pleaded guilty to Assault in the Third Degree, a misdemeanor. Because I had no prior record and no one was injured, I was given three years' probation, but the order of protection remained in effect. The judge who sentenced me emphasized the danger of violating the protection order, which prohibited me from going anywhere near my wife, the kids or the house they lived in, which just happened to be my house as well. I couldn't believe it. I was prevented from entering my own home or visiting with my kids. To make things worse, the order was to remain in force for six months.

I rented an apartment and was advised by my attorney that the fastest way to get things back to normal would be to reach an agreement with Maria. I immediately agreed to split everything down the middle. Actually I ended up with the house and she ended up with about a half million dollars in cash. However, I absolutely refused to allow her to take the kids with her to California. At one point I offered to let her take Maggie if I could keep Patrick. When she refused I instructed my attorney to demand an immediate custody hearing.

Thirty days later the family court judge rendered her decision in the case of Maria Alvarez-McShane vs. Paul William McShane. Patrick was ten, Maggie was nine and Larkin was twenty-six.

The clerk of the court rapped his gavel.

"Hear ye, hear ye, this court is now in session, Honorable Rebecca Neuman-Hicks presiding. All rise."

As Judge Neuman-Hicks re-entered the courtroom, I turned and looked at the clock. Eighteen minutes had passed since she had adjourned the case in order to render her decision. Only an hour-and-a-half of court time had been devoted to the question of custody.

After reading into the record all of the pertinent factual data such as our names, and dates of birth, to assure everyone that she really knew which case she was deciding . . . ours would be the third case she had decided that day . . . she finally reached the issue of which parent would have custody of Patrick and Maggie. My attorney was optimistic because on cross examination Maria had conceded that I was a devoted and caring father. She testified that she had accepted a position as a set designer for Millennium Films and it was her intention to go to California with Larkin who was joining a small documentary film company. It was their plan to marry as soon as her divorce was granted. Finally she admitted that she and Larkin did cocaine on occasion and that they had been engaged in a sexually intimate relationship for over six months before our breakup.

Judge Neuman-Hicks settled back in her high-backed leather chair, poured herself a glass of water from a pitcher on her desk, put on her spectacles, picked up a sheaf of papers, glanced at them, appeared to make a few notations on the papers, and finally looked down upon us. I leaned forward to make certain I wouldn't miss a word she said.

"After reviewing all the evidence in this tragic case," the Judge said solemnly, "I find that both parents are eminently qualified to assume custody and control of the minor children Patrick and Margaret." For a fleeting second I had this mad, wonderful thought that the judge was going to order Maria to stop loving Larkin and resume loving me.

"But that is not the problem here . . . " the judge continued. "The issue here is that the plaintiff intends to move to California and pursue a new career in the film industry with her paramour, soon to be her husband, and to take the children with her. The defendant vigorously opposes this plan because he claims that by doing so his wife will have effectively terminated his rights and privileges as a father; that because of the three thousand miles that would separate him from his children, he would be unfairly denied the opportunity to love and nurture them."

I was exhilarated. The judge had stated my

position exactly. "Right on, Judge!" I whispered under my breath.

"I am asked by these parties, in the image of Solomon, to choose one of them to be the sole custodian of these lovely children. I have personally spoken to both children, and it is crystal clear to me that they love both parents equally. Although they say their father is strict with them, they assured me that he was always fair, and they believed that he always tried to do what he thought was best for them. They indicated that their mother did not spend as much time with them, but she was always available to them when they needed her and she was a loving, caring parent. They indicated that their father was "old fashioned," to use their term, but I don't find that to be a negative character trait." I was ecstatic. The judge hesitated, looked up from her written text, poured herself more water, glanced over at both of us with a pained expression, and continued to deliver her decision.

"During the dark ages of family law, custody of minor children who had not reached puberty was automatically granted to the wife, but such is no longer the rule in this court." I heard Maria gasp. I dared not look over at her.

"At that time it was axiomatic that the wife and children would continue to reside in the same community as the husband so that he could fully exercise his rights of visitation. In those days he was usually the breadwinner and sole support of the wife and children. For better or worse, times have changed, and the law has been modified accordingly." I shifted uneasily in my chair.

"The husband in this case acknowledges that his wife is a competent, caring mother, but he asserts that custody of the children should be awarded to him because he is also a competent and caring father, and if the wife, to suit her own purposes, chooses to move to California and is allowed to take the children with her, she will be depriving him of his parental rights. Obviously he has failed to consider that if the children remain with him here in Rochester, New York, his wife will be deprived of her parental rights when she travels to California to pursue her career objectives. Should the court require her to sacrifice her career in order to preserve her relationship with her children? Has the husband considered sacrificing his career by moving to California in order to preserve his rights of visitation?

"I became satisfied that where the parties chose to live should not be a determinative factor in this case and therefore I decided I must look more closely at the character of the parties."

I felt as if I were on a roller coaster. Surely she could not find fault with my character, whereas Maria had been engaging in an illicit extramarital affair with Steiner for over six months.

"In my search, I found the report of the law guardian, appointed by the court to provide background information, to be most helpful. From his report I learned the details of the marriage and the circumstances surrounding the separation of the parties. "The husband urges me to consider the fact that the wife has been engaged in an adulterous relationship which she has openly admitted here in court, but I find no correlation between the commission of adultery and the ability to care for one's children. I am not here to punish anyone or to determine why this marriage failed. My sole responsibility is to decide how the interests of the children of the marriage can best be served. In all respects but one, I find the husband and wife equally qualified to undertake the sole custody of the children. Unfortunately, there is a flaw in the husband's character which can not be ignored. It is the potential for violence. A man who is capable of smashing in the door of his wife's bedroom with a baseball bat is demonstrably incapable of controlling his emotions. Granted he was provoked by his wife's decision to leave him for a younger man; granted he had been drinking, which may explain but never excuse his conduct . . . but . . . *no one has the right to engage in violence to influence or resolve a marital dispute!*

"In considering all the circumstances of this case, I hereby grant custody of Patrick and Margaret to their mother, the plaintiff, with the usual rights of visitation to the father, the defendant. The father shall have the children with him every other weekend; one evening during the off week; one month during the summer school vacation period and alternate Christmas holidays, subject always to whatever best serves the interests of the children.

"I am not unmindful of the fact that the plaintiff and the children may be living thousands of miles away from the defendant and I therefore decree that in such event, the father shall have the children with him during the months of July and August and during the Christmas holidays each year. Whenever the defendant-father is able to visit the children at their home in California or wherever plaintiff-mother may choose to live, the children shall reside with the father for the duration of his visit."

The judge rapped her gavel and quickly left the courtroom. I was devastated.

Maria's lawyer pumped his fist in the air, but she ignored him. She came over and slid into the chair beside me.

"Paul," she whispered.

I turned away from her, wiping my eyes with my handkerchief.

"I couldn't help what happened," she said. "I tried. Larkin and I both tried to prevent it from happening, but it was beyond us. You were the first man I ever loved. It's just that . . . " She reached over and put her hand on my sleeve. I stood up. I couldn't look at her.

"Goodbye, Paul," she said softly, and walked quickly from the room.

I sat in that silent courtroom, all alone, trying to sort things out. I understood what had happened to Maria. After all, I was not a stranger to young love. Even if I had known about her affair with Larkin I knew I could not have prevented her from pursuing it. Reason and logic are incompatible with passion, but, Oh Lord I cried, I have lost the *blood of my blood* and the *flesh of my flesh* and I don't know how I can bear it.

I stayed in the courtroom until the custodian finally came and told me I would have to leave. I walked aimlessly from the courthouse and entered the first bar I came to.

"Where's my car parked?" I mumbled.

"Sorry, pops, I can't let you drive tonight. I'll call a cab." The bartender picked up the phone and dialed. I started to protest, but I couldn't remember what I was protesting. The taxi dropped me off in front of my house. I stumbled up the front path and took the elevator up to my apartment, but I couldn't fit the key in the lock. So I spent what was left of the night sleeping in the hallway. I awakened with the sun shining in my eyes. I ached all over, and my head felt as if it were stuffed with salamanders. I had consumed my fair share of alcohol in my life, but I had never drunk myself into oblivion before.

I worked in my apartment all the following week, unable to face my colleagues, and their condolences.

When Maria left for California with the kids two days after she was awarded custody, I moved back into our house, but without all of them around me, the echo of my footsteps was the only evidence of my existence. Every corner was filled with memories. The crack in the dining room window from Patrick's "home run" in our back-yard world series . . . the stain on the living room carpet where he had knocked over the can of yellow paint . . . the saw marks on the coffee table where he had experimented with my hacksaw when he was three years old . . . the hole we made in the screen door so that Maggie's cat could come and go as he pleased. . . .

I went into deep depression. I couldn't eat, I couldn't sleep, and work was out of the question. I continued to drink heavily and refused to talk to the few friends I had left. Each day I thought I would snap out of it, but the torment didn't stop. And then one morning several weeks later as I poured myself my first drink of the day, a slim volume entitled *Courage* caught my eye, leaning askew on the bookshelf above my desk. The inscription on the flyleaf read "To Paul from Dad, April 3, 1943." It was my sixteenth birthday present from my father.

The book was a collection of short biographies of American men and women who had overcome adversity through hard work, dedication and tenacity: Abraham Lincoln, Helen

Keller, Booker T. Washington, Franklin Delano Roosevelt and many other lesser known men and women who refused to give up despite their handicaps.

I flipped through the pages. My eye caught a phrase in the chapter devoted to Helen Keller. "I knew only darkness and stillness . . . my life was without past or future . . . my hand clutched of emptiness."

I closed the book and thought for a moment. "I am not blind and I am not deaf, I am just a drunk."

I smashed the bottle of whiskey against the wall and slumped in my chair. The judge's decision lay on the top of desk where I had thrown it after ripping it to pieces. I started to fit the pieces together. . . . The words leaped out at me. . . . "Whenever the defendant-father is able to visit the children at their home in California or wherever the plaintiff-mother may choose to live, the children shall reside with the father for the duration of his visit." I remembered what else the judge had said when she gave her decision "Has the husband considered sacrificing his career by moving to California to be with his children?"

I picked up the phone and called my junior partner at the office.

"Hello, Chuck? I've got to see you right away. I'll be in the office in twenty minutes." I hung up the phone, jumped in my car and headed downtown. By six o'clock Chuck and I had reached an agreement for him to buy out my interest in the partnership within sixty days.

I figured that the demand for sixty-five-year-old architects in California was probably about the same as the demand for sixty-five-year-old go-go dancers, but during the ensuing months I was able to line up a few interviews and I was optimistic. I mean what the hell, Michelangelo designed the dome of St. Peter's Basilica in Rome when he was eighty-five and Frank Lloyd Wright was eighty-nine when he designed the Guggenheim Museum in New York City.

As soon as the sale of the house was completed, I rented a big van, loaded every blessed thing I owned into it and headed west. When I crossed the state line, it was without regrets. I traveled Route 90 to Cleveland, Route 80 to Chicago, Des Moines, Omaha and Cheyenne. Then I went south to Denver and continued on to Albuquerque. I took my time, occasionally stopping along the way to see the sights, so it was almost two weeks before I saw the sign "Los Angeles 397 miles."

I had done my homework and had learned a lot about Santa Barbara where Maria and the kids were living, but I wasn't prepared for how absolutely beautiful the area was. I was overwhelmed by the sight of the thousands of acres of flowers in bloom. Van Gogh immediately came to mind and I had the feeling that the scene was imitating him instead of the other way around. I discovered a lovely country inn on the outskirts of the city and rented a car for a few days so that I could scout around a bit. I located Maria's home without any difficulty and was selfishly pleased to find that it was a ranch style "tract" house in a subdivision where all the houses looked a little different but in fact were exactly the same. I thought briefly about which of the windows looked out from Maria and Larkin's bedroom. My vision of them sharing the master bedroom caused me to grip the steering wheel so tight that my knuckles turned white. I peeled rubber to get away and calm down.

On the following day, I located Patrick and Maggie's school. It was nice, very nice. I wondered if going to school with palm trees in the playground had an effect upon how you perceived life as an adolescent. At 2:45 I positioned myself so that I could see the kids as they emerged from the school building and headed for the bus. I saw Maggie first and my heart began to thump. God, she was a beautiful child. She was carrying a number of books cradled in her arms and was chattering away with a group of girls who climbed onto the bus together. She looked healthy, happy, and without a care. "That's good," I thought. Then I spotted Patrick. He was walking alone and looked despondent.

I wanted to rush over to him and pick him up in my arms, but I didn't. "Patience," I thought. "I must be patient."

I spent the following day looking for a place to live. I had just about given up finding what I wanted when a place turned up that was perfect for my needs. It was a small unfurnished three-bedroom cottage located on a quiet street in the old part of town. The rent was steep, but it was within easy walking distance of the subdivision where Maria and the kids lived and was immediately available. I signed a year's lease on the spot.

Within the next few days I completed my interviews and was lucky to find a position with a dynamic group of young architects who had more work than they could handle. My ten years' experience in Arizona turned the trick for me and though I would be taking home a paycheck that was dramatically less than I had been making, it was fair and adequate under the circumstances. After selling the house back in Rochester and giving up my interest in the firm, I had plenty of money in the bank and I knew that my true value as an architect would be appreciated by my new employers as soon as I had a chance to show them what I could do. I wasn't over the hill by a long shot.

Although I had originally intended to just turn up on Maria's doorstep and surprise them all, I decided it would be better if I called and gave warning of my arrival. My hand trembled as I dialed their number.

"Hi. I'm sorry we aren't home right now, but if you will leave your name and number we'll call you back as soon as possible." It was Maggie on the answering machine.

I was thrilled to hear her voice again. It had been almost a month since I had spoken to the kids. I put on my "U.S. Open" tennis shirt that Maggie had given me on my last birthday, and the cap Patrick gave me inscribed, "Paul McShane–Champ." I had turned in my van and rented a Jeep Wrangler, which was Patrick's favorite set of wheels. I drove over to their house. I walked up the sidewalk and rang the bell, holding my breath as I waited. When no one answered I rapped with the brass knocker but there was still no answer. I walked around to the back door and knocked again. I peered in the window. I looked in the garage and discovered that it was empty. My shoulders sagged with disappointment as I returned to my car prepared to wait for as long as it took. I wasn't going to miss them no matter what. After two hours of waiting a station wagon pulled into the driveway, immediately followed by a pickup driven by Larkin. The children jumped out of the wagon and ran into the house. As Maria stepped out of the car, Larkin joined her. They kissed briefly and then he draped his arm around her shoulders as they walked slowly around to the back of the house. I could scarcely breathe. I was in turmoil. I wondered if I had misjudged everything. They looked like a happy young couple with two kids. Would I be an unwelcome intrusion . . . an embarrassment to everyone. He looked so young, like a normal, attractive young husband and father. I found the weight of my sixty-five years oppressive and wondered if my plan to resurrect my relationship with the children was a farce, created by my ego and driven by the belief that I could not be replaced . . . that I was their natural father with such a deep love for them that no other man could walk in my shoes. But I had come too far to turn back. I got out of the car and walked up the path to the front door. I rang the doorbell and waited, hoping that Larkin would not be the one to open the door. As I started to ring the bell a second time, the door swung open. It was Maggie.

"Dad," she screamed and leaped into my arms. We smothered each other with kisses. Then Patrick showed up and he was punching me on the arm, laughing hysterically and trying to pull me away from Maggie. He managed to push me into the foyer where he jumped on my back. I lost my balance and the three of us went down in a heap on the floor in a tumbled mass of arms and legs and wondrous laughter. Maria came rushing out from the kitchen to investigate the cause of the ruckus. It was a bit awkward trying to greet her while lying on my back with Maggie sitting on my chest and Patrick holding my head in an arm lock. Since Patrick was sprawled across my face, Maria had no idea who I was. She confessed later that at first she thought I was a burglar that the children had heroically subdued.

"Paul!" she exclaimed as she pulled the kids off of me. "What are you doing here?"

"I just came to say hello," I stammered, smiling sheepishly. I thought I would explode from the joy of seeing her again. Although she had gained weight, she looked as lovely as ever. The California sun had darkened her color to a rich mahogany and she was dressed in gypsy colors with accents of Mexican silver. Larkin joined the group and was staring at me quizzically.

"What's up?" he asked nonchalantly.

"It's Paul," Maria answered quickly. "He just came to say hello."

"What is he doing on the floor?" Larkin asked. It was becoming awkward. I felt very foolish and didn't know what to do because I wasn't able to just spring up without help. Although I was in good shape for my age, I would first have to roll up on my hands and knees and I didn't want the kids to see me getting up that way, especially in front of Larkin.

"The children thought Paul was an intruder and knocked him down," Maria said.

"That's not exactly what happened," I interjected, still trying to find a way to stand up without making a big deal of it.

"No, no!" Patrick and Maggie squealed in

chorus. "We didn't mean to knock him down." I don't know if Maria recognized my plight, but God bless her, she held out her hand which I took gratefully and scrambled to my feet uneventfully.

"Welcome to California," she said. "How about a drink?"

"Sounds great to me," I replied, putting an arm around each kid as Larkin turned and left the room without saying another word. Maria led the procession into the tiny living room, indicating that I should sit in the large overstuffed chair that dominated the room. Maggie immediately curled up at my feet and Patrick lounged nonchalantly against the back of my chair. Maggie looked spectacular, with Maria's jet black hair, my blue eyes and her lithe young body burnished by California sunshine. Patrick seemed to have grown taller during the five months that had passed since I had last seen him, and the way he had his hair cut he could easily have passed for one of the local Mexican kids.

When Maria returned with my favorite drink she had changed into a white maternity shift which accented her dark complexion. "My God, they're going to have a baby!" I gasped under my breath. My hopes, buried in the deep recesses of my mind, that perhaps one day Maria would tire of Larkin and come home to me, were dashed to pieces. She must have observed the shock on my face because she immediately said, "I wrote to tell you that Larkin and I are, you know . . . going to have a child in October. Perhaps my letter arrived after you left Rochester."

"Perhaps," I replied, reaching out to take my drink from her, averting my eyes and trying to regain my composure. "Congratulations," I said, raising my glass. When I dared to look at her again, I found her absolutely stunning. Perhaps it was the glow of pregnancy that made her so appealing to me. The last time I had seen her, after all, was in a cold courtroom at one of the worst moments of my life. I had difficulty ignoring the effect she was having on me. If the children hadn't been there to remind me of the purpose of my visit I would have probably made a fool of myself. Maggie saved the day by asking me all kinds of questions like where I was living, how long I was going to stay in California and whether I would take them out for pizza and ice cream.

"It all depends upon your mother," I said, glancing hopefully at Maria.

"Can we Mom, please, can we?" Maggie pleaded.

"Well I haven't started dinner yet, I can't see why not," she said smiling. "You haven't seen your father in a long time, and I'm sure you have a lot to tell him about life in sunny California."

"You mean 'smoggy' California," Patrick chided.

"C'mon now, it's not that bad," Maria said defensively.

"Oh yeah. Then how come the school bus driver wears scuba gear every day when he picks us up?"

"Yeah Mom, how come?" Maggie chimed in.

Maria said, "You can take your snorkeling equipment with you to the pizza parlor if you want to." I loved it. I loved every minute of it. The bantering and the giggling and the silly jokes. I wanted it to go on and on. Their voices tumbled through my mind like a musical score . . . Maria's rich contralto with just the faintest remnants of her Latin heritage, Maggie's lilting soprano and Patrick filling in between with a voice that couldn't make up its mind where it belonged.

"Let's go, Dad, before we get another earthquake and they close down the pizza place," Maggie said with a straight face.

"We could always pick up some pot at the grocery store," Patrick said looking equally serious.

"That's not funny, young man," Maria scolded.

"If the store's closed we could get some from Larkin," Maggie added. I could see things were getting out of hand. Before Maria had a chance to say a word I spoke as if I hadn't heard Maggie. "I hope you and Larkin can join us," I lied.

"He has to go back to the studio," Maria replied apologetically.

"I'd love to have you come with us," I said. I could tell that Maria was apprehensive, but she agreed to come along.

"Kapowee kazam!" Maggie shrieked, pulling her mother and me out of the house and down the front path.

"My car is right over there," I said, pointing to my Jeep Wrangler.

"Cool, man!" Patrick exclaimed.

"Wow! Can we put the top down, Dad? Please, Daddy, *please*," Maggie begged. I glanced at Maria. She was smiling and appeared to be caught up in the frivolity of the moment, so I agreed. Patrick helped me fold it down and we headed off to Botticelli's, Patrick's favorite restaurant, for pizza.

"He just likes it because they have all these dumb naked lady statues," Maggie said.

"Shut up!" Patrick snapped.

"It's true and you know it."

"You better shut up, motor mouth."

"That's quite enough out of both of you," Maria said grimly, while I tried to keep from laughing. Patrick took a half-hearted swing at Maggie, who screamed, "Daddy, don't let him hit me," and then poked Patrick in the ribs when her mother wasn't looking.

"Owwww," Patrick yelled, grabbing Maggie's hair.

"Now that's enough. If you two don't cut it out your father is going to drive us right back home . . . and I mean it!"

The kids knew when Maria was serious, and we rode in silence for a few minutes.

"How would you like a couple of juvenile delinquents?" Maria demanded, still fuming.

"I'd like it a lot," I replied quickly.

"I didn't mean it that way," Maria said turning red in the face.

"I know, I know . . . I was only kidding . . . well . . . not really . . . but you know . . . " I quickly changed the subject. "I love nude lady statues, but how is the food?" I quipped, turning my head in Patrick's direction.

"Fab, Dad, really fab."

Botticelli's was indeed "fab." It featured an outdoor olive garden surrounded by every classic female nude statue known to man. There were also a number of nude male statues, to be politically correct, I suppose, and overall, with its olive vines, arches, pillars, and fountains, it was standard California "excess." Of course the real reason I loved it was that we were all together again. It was the best dinner I had had in months and I have no idea what the food tasted like.

Apparently it was their custom to allow the kids to walk down the road a bit to a "Tastee Freeze" for their ice cream while the adults had after dinner drinks, so I ordered a B&B for me and an Amaretto on the rocks for Maria. After the drinks arrived I settled back, wondering how to tell Maria what I had in mind.

"The children have been with you for five months, one week and three days." Maria refused to look at me as I described how much I missed the kids, how much they meant to me, how important they were in my life. I told her that I had sold the house, and had given up my practice in New York so that I could move to California to be near the children. Finally she turned to me.

"What is this leading up to? If you are really

going to live out here for a while, I don't see any problem with following the court order, I mean . . . the kids would be with you every other weekend." She looked at me warily and finished off her drink. I signaled the waiter for another round, giving me a little more time to summon the courage to put all of my cards on the table. We sat in uneasy silence again until the waiter showed up with our drinks. Then I slipped a copy of the judge's order out of my pocket and slid it across the table to her. I had highlighted the words which had prompted me to move, lock, stock and barrel to California. "WHENEVER THE FATHER IS ABLE TO VISIT THE CHILDREN AT THEIR HOME IN CALIFORNIA THEY SHALL RESIDE WITH THE FATHER FOR THE DURATION OF HIS VISIT."

Maria picked up the legal document, stared at it, read it and reread it. I noticed a slight trembling in her hands when she put the sheet of paper back on the table. "It doesn't mean what I know you're thinking." She looked up at me defiantly. "I can't agree to let you have them. I'm their mother and . . . "

"I'm their father. You broke up our home, you—"

"I fell in love. Can't you understand that?"

"No, damn it, I can't."

"I fell in love with someone who—"

"Who what?" I demanded, raising my voice in anger.

"Someone who was my own age. Now do you understand it? Oh my God," she wailed, covering her face with her hands. I was stunned. I thought to myself, "I am an old man and I can't accept it. I don't think like an old man, I don't talk like an old man or walk like an old man, but she's right . . . compared to her and Larkin, I am an old man." She was sobbing and I wanted to reach out and comfort her. I wanted her to reach out and comfort me. Then there was a commotion at the front of the restaurant that drew everyone's attention. Maggie came running up to our table, screaming.

"Dad, Dad, Patrick has been hit by a car. Mom, Patrick's hurt bad, I think he's dead!" The three of us ran out of the restaurant. A few hundred feet from the entrance a crowd had gathered, I pushed my way through and found Patrick lying inert on the ground. He was covered with blood which was gushing from a jagged laceration in his forehead. His right leg was askew, with a portion of bone protruding through the skin. I felt his pulse. He was alive!

His pulse was very weak. I ripped off my shirt and pressed it tight against the open wound to try and staunch the flow of blood. "911," I screamed. "Did anyone call 911?" A young man holding a cell phone to his ear said, "They're on their way. They said not to move him." Someone brought a blanket and handed it to me. Maria knelt down on the other side of Patrick and we covered him gently with the blanket just as the ambulance arrived. I followed alongside the stretcher as the paramedics eased him into the back of the ambulance.

"I'm his father," I said anxiously.

"Hop in," the driver said, indicating the seat beside him.

"Where are we going? "I asked.

"St. Joe's," he replied, as the siren began to wail. I caught sight of Maria and Maggie as we backed up and then nosed out on to the busy highway. I leaned out the window and yelled, "St. Joe's!" When I looked into the back of the ambulance I saw that the Medic was giving Patrick oxygen. When we arrived at the hospital they immediately took him to the operating room. I felt so helpless. My son's life was in the hands of total strangers and I knew that the best thing I could do was to stay out of everyone's way.

By the time Maria and Maggie arrived I had learned that Patrick had a severe fracture of his right leg and undetermined internal injuries. It was the internal injuries that were creating the greatest concern. He had profuse internal bleeding that required immediate abdominal surgery. They discovered a lacerated spleen that required a massive blood transfusion and Maria and I immediately offered to contribute blood. They did a preliminary test to make certain we did not carry any virus that could be harmful, and we waited anxiously for the results so they could approve us as donors to help save our son's life. I was a bit anxious about Maria giving blood when she was pregnant and I wondered if my blood was too old to be worth anything. After about a half hour I walked over to the nurse's station to try and find out what was going on.

"Excuse me," I said, "Can you fill me in on what's happening with Patrick McShane?

"Yes sir," she replied. "He needed special blood, which they had to requisition from the blood bank, but it arrived in time and he's going to be just fine."

"Why didn't they take my blood or his mother's? Is there something wrong with it?"

"No, but you and your daughter, Maria,

have blood type A which isn't compatible with Patrick's. He's type B."

"She's not my . . . I mean he's my. . . . "

"Excuse me sir, I'll be right back," the nurse said, scurrying away in response to a call on the loud speaker.

"That's ridiculous," I thought. "If Maria and I have type A blood, Patrick can't have type B blood. I'm not a biochemist but I'm smart enough to figure that out. They must have made a mistake . . . unless . . . "

"What did she say?" Maria asked anxiously.

"He's going to be all right," I mumbled.

"Gracias, Dios." she whispered, and then clung to me sobbing quietly. I held her stiffly in my arms until she gained control of herself, and then I left her in the visitors lounge and walked down the deserted corridor. What does it all mean, I asked myself. "I have a nine-year-old son that I love more than life itself and now I learn that he is probably not my son. He can't be my son. No, *he is my son but I am not his father.*" I tried not to think about who the father might be, and the fact that Maria must have known about it all along. The pieces began to fall into place. Maria's apartment back in Rochester when we made love for the first time. She was not a stranger to the art of passion; she had surrounded her living space with an aura of eroticism; we had engaged in wild, hard-driving sex with abandon . . . *because she knew she was already pregnant.* Patrick's *premature* birth wasn't premature at all. Then I wondered if she chose me as the father of her child only for financial security, or could it be that she thought I would be the best father she could provide for her child. Patrick's biological father probably didn't even know he was a father. He was just a participant in a few minutes of unprotected sex, depositing his seed in a fertile vault. So, did that make him Patrick's father? "No fucking way," I cried aloud, "*Paul McShane* is the father of Patrick McShane!"

I was alone in the room with him when his eyelids fluttered for the first time. I held his small hand in mine as he slowly emerged from the anesthetic.

"Patrick," I whispered.

"Dad, where am I? What happened?" At that moment a nurse came in the room accompanied by Maria.

"Mom," Patrick said, as she took his other hand, tears streaming down her cheeks.

We sat through the night with him until we were certain that he was out of danger.

At ten o'clock the following morning the nurse suggested we leave for a while. Maria had been unable to locate Larkin after the accident, so she had left a message for him and arranged for Maggie to spend the night with a girlfriend who lived a few houses down the street. She tried calling Larkin again in the morning at the studio. Whoever answered the phone at his office told Maria that he was in an important meeting and couldn't be disturbed. She replied, "Tell him it is his wife calling and that I must speak to him right away." I guess Larkin left a message that he would call her when he had a chance, and the person hung up the phone. Maria's anger got lost amidst her anxiety about Patrick, but I understood how she felt. Larkin didn't learn about the accident until the next day and then he didn't show up at the hospital until several days later.

I spent every hour that I could with Patrick. Each day I was there when he awakened and I watched him close his eyes in sleep each night. I couldn't look at Maria. We hardly spoke to each other. One day when we were standing in the hall outside his room she asked me why I was avoiding her. I thought of our conversation eleven years earlier in Hooligan's bar when she had asked the same question. I thought I wouldn't be able to look at her ever again without remembering her treachery. But like flesh wounds, a heart will mend if given a chance.

"I'm not," I lied, "I've just been worried about Patrick."

After a few weeks our relationship returned to normal, or at least as close to normal as possible under the circumstances.

"So how is my favorite patient doing today?" nurse Campbell said each morning when she brought Patrick's breakfast to him. Erin Campbell was not only a spectacular nurse but also a bright and attractive woman. She and I had lunch together in the cafeteria a few times during Patrick's first few weeks in the hospital and then as the days passed we had fallen into a routine in which I would meet her there on her breaks whenever I could. She was a widow who had moved from Madison, Wisconsin, after her husband died of a heart attack at age fifty-five. Since both of her children lived in California she decided to get away from the difficult winters and spend more time with her son and daughter and her grandchildren. We joked about the fact that her oldest grandson was only five years younger than Patrick. At first we talked mostly about Patrick, but as time passed we slid very comfortably into exchanging life stories and our dreams for the future. I found myself anxiously looking forward to our time together each day and was amused to discover that I was always a bit depressed on her days off. I soon realized that she had become a pleasant part of my daily routine. On a whim I decided to invite her to join me for dinner.

"I'm sorry, Paul, Danny planned this evening weeks ago. We have tickets to a revival of *Man of La Mancha,* which is one of my all-time favorites."

"Danny? Who is Danny?" I demanded. Erin flushed.

"Danny is one of my gentleman friends. I do have a life outside St. Joseph's Hospital, you know," she replied, smiling a bit sheepishly, I thought.

"You never told me about Danny," I said accusingly.

"I don't recall that you ever told me about any of your lady friends either," she said, continuing to smile in a way that I found most disconcerting.

"It's just that once I got up the courage to invite you out—" I shrugged my shoulders in a gesture of helplessness.

"Now now, Paul it can't be all that bad.

Besides, to be totally fair here, do you always invite your guests to dinner on the afternoon of the event? I mean, suppose I wanted to have something new to wear on such a special occasion? Part of the fun, you know, is getting ready for a date."

"Of course I should not have waited until the last moment to invite you, and I guess we don't know each other well enough to just do something spontaneously."

"You can invite me to do something spontaneously any time. I love spur-of-the moment adventures . . . when I'm free to enjoy them. It just so happens that tonight I'm committed."

"Okay, how about tomorrow night?"

"Oh dear," she wailed.

"Well then, let me put it this way. When are you available?"

"A week from next Friday?" she suggested.

"Are you serious?" I stammered. "Are you telling me that you don't have a single night open until ten days from now?"

"Dear Paul, I think you have been away from the 'singles' scene a long time, or maybe it's just different for us ladies. We fill up our dance cards far enough in advance so that we are only alone when we choose to be."

"I'm impressed. Sad, but impressed," I sighed. "All right, a week from Friday it is. Theater and dinner after. And formal by God. I mean it, black tie, the works."

"I love it. You've got yourself a date."

And so my first affair in eleven years began. I had forgotten how exciting and enervating the chase can be. Frustrating too, because Erin was not about to give up her way of life just because I happened on the scene; and her other male friends didn't disappear when I walked through the door. I don't know how much of my desire to be with her was involved with the challenge of easing her away from her other suitors, and how much of it was based upon a growing affection for her. The fact of the matter was that we were having a wonderful time together. I hadn't played tennis in years, but she got me back on the courts, and after a few weeks I was able to play well enough to hold my own and was invited to join in her Wednesday night round robin tournaments.

Whereas the highlight of my days at the hospital used to be Maria's daily visits, I discovered that whenever Erin's breaks and Maria's time at the hospital coincided I would leave Patrick and Maria together and slip down to the cafeteria to be with Erin. I had no idea where my relationship with Erin was headed, but I knew I didn't want it to end when Patrick was discharged from the hospital.

After the first two weeks, the tubes and other medical paraphernalia were removed and Patrick's pain was under control. Finally, the doctor told us that Patrick could go home. Since the children were supposed to be with me during the months of July and August, I didn't have to battle with Maria. We had studiously avoided any further conversation about custody since our confrontation at the restaurant just before Patrick's accident.

On the day Patrick was being discharged, Maria whispered to me that she wanted to speak to me alone. I met her at the outside terrace.

"Larkin is involved in shooting a film on location in Brazil. He says he wants me to come with him, but with Patrick still convalescing and with me being pregnant . . . "

"I would be happy to take the kids while you're gone," I offered, holding my breath.

"We'll be away for at least six months."

"I'm sure we would be able to manage things," I said confidently.

"Larkin isn't as enthusiastic about the baby

as I would like, and maybe he would think differently about it if we were alone for a while. He and Patrick don't get along so well, you know."

"I didn't know," I said gently.

"Oh, it isn't anything serious, its just that I think they haven't worked things out between themselves yet. As you may have seen, Patrick is reaching that difficult time when he tries to appear grown up, but inside he is still a very young boy. Most of the time he isn't very nice to Larkin."

"It takes time. That's pretty common at his age I suspect," I offered, masking my delight in learning that Larkin hadn't taken my place in Patrick's life.

"It would be good for you too, Paul, don't you think?"

"I suspect it probably would," I replied, trying desperately to keep the overwhelming joy I felt from showing. Maria reached in her handbag and pulled out a pack of Virginia Slims. She lit up, inhaled deeply and let the smoke drift out slowly between her lips.

"I didn't know you had started smoking again," I said cautiously.

"I don't very often, especially now that I'm pregnant, although Larkin doesn't seem to mind. He never hassles me about it the way you always did." She smiled. I winced inwardly when she took a deep drag on her cigarette and dropped it on the floor, stamping it out with the toe of her shoe.

"I'll call you tomorrow," she said. Then she draped her jacket over her shoulders, stepped close to me, caressed my cheek with her fingertips, brushed her lips across mine and turned away. The staccato beat of her high heels striking the tile floor as she walked briskly down the deserted hospital corridor lingered on long after she had gone.

Maria and Larkin sold their home, which Maria had paid for. Larkin invested the proceeds of the sale along with everything else Maria had received in the divorce settlement in his film venture. They were required to turn over possession of their home to the buyer within a few days, so we had to hustle to pack up all of the kids' clothing and other treasures, and move them into my place. During the process I gathered that Maria's relationship with Larkin had deteriorated very rapidly after their move to California. It seemed that having two kids thrust into the midst of their love affair was not a simple problem for any of them to handle. Since

Larkin was six years younger than Maria, with no parenting experience, a volatile environment was created which was beyond Maria's ability to control.

There were tears on the day Maria came to say goodbye, not unlike those that were shed when they all moved to California, but she assured the children that she would return in six months to have her baby in the States even if Larkin's film wasn't completed by that time.

"Then we will all be together again," she said to the kids, "and you will have a new little brother or sister."

I decided to worry about that complication when the time came, and planned to structure my life in such a way as to take the greatest joy possible from each passing hour.

During the last two weeks in August we rented an RV and drove up along the coast to Seattle and then took the ferry over to Victoria Island in British Columbia. One night on our way back home we discovered a tiny isolated cove on the coast of Oregon. We set up camp and cooked steaks on an open fire. It was a warm night and the sky was awash with stars. After dinner we sat around gazing into the fire, content with our own thoughts. I wanted the trip to go on forever, but I could tell the kids were anxious to head back home to their friends. Maggie interrupted my reverie with a remark that sent me into a tailspin.

"Mom told me in her last letter that the baby is due right after Christmas," she said enthusiastically. I didn't know how to respond to Maggie. I was trying to think the whole thing through when Patrick stood up, threw another small log on the fire and said in a soft voice, "I'm not going back to live with them. I'm staying with Dad." Then he walked slowly down to the beach and began skipping stones across the dark water. I glanced over at Maggie. The moonlight was casting shadows across her face. I watched a tear slide down her cheek.

"I don't know what to do, Daddy," she sobbed. "I love you both, but Mom says she's counting on me to help her with the baby, and she says she misses me something awful and I miss her so much . . . " And then she was in my arms.

"Of course you do," I said, holding her tight. "We all love each other, but it got messed up somehow . . . " I stroked her hair. I didn't know how to continue.

"I want it to be like it used to be," Maggie said, "before smelly old Larkin showed up."

I did my best not to smile, but I didn't succeed, and then Maggie stopped crying and started to giggle and everything was okay again.

When we got back home and finished unloading the RV, I mixed myself a drink and walked out front to gather up the mail. There were no letters from Maria, but I received a card from Erin. The card had a drawing of a man standing beside his mailbox with a large garbage container beside him labeled "JUNK MAIL." The inscription inside said, "DON'T YOU DARE!" with her handwritten note, "Thinking of you . . . fondly, Erin." I decided to invite her to join us for dinner on Saturday night.

The dinner was a complete disaster. It was supposed to be a garden party but it poured rain all day and night. I attempted to grill the steaks on the back porch and the porch ceiling began to smolder. I immediately grabbed the fire extinguisher and succeeded in spraying foam all over the steaks. Maggie and Patrick became embroiled in an argument over which television program to watch. It ended with Maggie stomping up to her room and slamming the door. Patrick decided he didn't want to watch television after all. He said he was going over to his friend's house. I said he couldn't go until after dinner. He said he wasn't hungry. I said I didn't much give a damn what he did and he left immediately. I called Maggie down to dinner. She said she wasn't hungry either. Erin smiled through it all, but I was angry and embarrassed by their behavior. I realized that Patrick and Maggie were not about to allow another "Larkin" into the family without a fight, but Erin was a bright, caring, gentle lady and Larkin was an immature, selfish, arrogant bastard. Erin pointed out to me that it would take time for her and the children to become friends and that I must be patient. She wisely suggested that we define our own relationship before she undertook the problem of dealing with my two teenagers. We spent the balance of the evening happily defining our relationship.

After the kids went back to school our lives became more hectic. When my new employers discovered the breadth of my experience they quickly gave me greater responsibility and more challenging work, but I found the role of a single working parent to be much more demanding than I had anticipated. Nevertheless we all sort of pulled together and somehow muddled through it. They were happy, rewarding days and Erin began to play an important role in all our lives. She was extremely sensitive to the situation with the children and within a very short time she had gained their affection and respect. I didn't know how it was all going to play out but I felt confident that we were heading in the right direction. When Patrick and Maggie invited Erin to help us cook the Thanksgiving turkey, I figured we had it made.

The Saint Catherine of Sienna Hospital in Rio de Janeiro operated above South American standards but far below the level of care one would expect to receive in the U.S.

Doctor Carmelita Estrada was the head of the Ob/Gyn department, and was a very competent physician. She and her young assistant examined the American female that she had been asked to evaluate. The patient was heavily sedated. The physician picked up her medical chart and read it over.

"Thirty-four years old, gestation period thirty-six weeks . . . contractions started 0800."

She glanced at her watch, it was 9:45. "She doesn't look good. Too pale," she said. She noted that she had been admitted to the hospital complaining of severe pain in the lower abdomen with increasing weakness. Her mind was racing.

"So Carlos, what do you think?"she asked her young colleague

"It's obvious that something is wrong, and with lower abdominal pain I would immediately suspect placenta abruptio but there is no evidence of bleeding," he replied.

"Maybe it is concealed . . . sometimes when the placenta separates from the uterus the blood flows behind the placenta . . . you can't see the bleeding . . . you can't be certain . . . an abdominal sonogram would probably tell the story, but our equipment isn't working . . . you see here, the fetal monitor indicates the fetal heart beat is variable . . . that's not good . . . the cervix is closed. . . . We don't have a lot of time on this one Doctor. Get her prepped for a c-section. Contact the next of kin for consent to surgery."

It was six o'clock in the morning when I received the call from the American Embassy.

"May I speak with Mr. Paul McShane, please," a strange voice demanded.

"Speaking. Who is this?" I asked, not quite awake.

"Juan Ramiriz, from the American Embassy in Rio de Janeiro."

"What is this about?" I asked anxiously.

"Mr. McShane, are you acquainted with Mrs. Larkin Steiner?

"Yes I am, I'm her former husband. Is anything wrong."

"I'm afraid so. You see, Mrs. Steiner is in the hospital here in critical condition. She requires immediate surgery and there is no one here to sign the necessary papers. Mrs. Steiner is in a coma and someone must sign to authorize the surgery. I'm advised by the doctor that Mrs. Steiner's life and the life of her unborn child are in jeopardy if surgery isn't performed immediately."

"Where's her husband?"

"That's the problem, sir, he left the country a few days ago and we haven't been able to track him down—"

"Never mind, of course I'll sign whatever is required. I can arrange to fax it to you immediately."

"Unfortunately there is also another matter: someone must be responsible for the costs. The surgery and the hospital, you know it is very expensive. They tell me it will cost at least two thousand dollars, maybe more."

"It doesn't matter, I will be responsible."

"All right then, if you wire transfer the money to the embassy here and send the consent by fax we will be able to take care of things at this end."

I immediately called Erin and discussed the situation with her. She thought I should consider flying to Rio. She said that as a nurse she had been witness to similar situations, usually with unwed mothers, and to be totally alone with no family support at such a time was a devastating experience. It would be doubly so, she said, with Maria being in a foreign country.

"But suppose by the time I arrive there, Larkin has returned," I argued

"Suppose he hasn't," she countered.

She offered to come and stay with the kids, and within four hours I was in the air on my way to Brazil.

By the time I arrived Maria had come through the surgery successfully and was off the critical list. She had given birth to a male child, Larkin Steiner, Jr. Larkin Steiner, Sr. remained unaccounted for.

When I entered the dismal hospital room, the shades were drawn. Maria was awake but still groggy. I stood in the doorway, blocking the only source of light in the room.

"Larkin," she whimpered, "Is the baby all right? Thank God you're here."

"Maria," I said softly. She knew something was amiss but she was unable to grasp what it was. "It's me, Paul." She stared up at me trying to focus, to understand.

"Paul?" she gasped. "What's wrong? Where's Larkin? Paul, what are you doing here?"

"There's nothing wrong. The baby is fine, but they haven't been able to find Larkin. If you point me in the right direction I'll do my best to locate him," I assured her. She started to sit up and then caught her breath from the pain. "Easy does it," I cautioned. "You're not quite ready for aerobics you know." She lay back down on the bed and looked up at me helplessly.

"I don't know where he is," she wailed.

I didn't know what to say or do. I sat through the night with her and the next day she told me what had happened.

"The major funding for the film didn't come through," she explained. "When my money ran out the project fell apart. Larkin and I were fighting all the time and then I discovered he had something going with Monica, the assistant director, and he began to stay away for days at a time. When we did see each other all we did was argue about money and Monica and . . . Oh God, Paul, it's such a mess." She started to sob softly. I just sort of stood there foolishly holding her hand. I told her to get some sleep and that I would be back in a few hours.

I wandered around the city trying to figure out what to do, and then decided to check out the American Embassy. I located Ramiriz there and he told me that Steiner and his crew had run up a mountain of debt and there were a lot of angry Brazilians looking for him. The immigration records disclosed that Larkin Steiner and Monica Reichart had departed a week earlier on a Lufthansa flight to Berlin.

"In English you say 'fly the coop,' I think, no?" Mr. Ramiriz asked me.

"Looks that way, I'm afraid, but maybe there is more to it than we know right now," I said.

"Maybe so," he said cheerfully.

Next I took a cab to Maria's apartment and ran into another hornet's nest. They were behind on the rent. I knew Maria was going to need a place to stay when she was discharged from the hospital, and the landlord was threatening to confiscate all of her possessions. I paid the back rent.

When she learned that Larkin had abandoned her, Maria went into a deep depression. I discovered that her telephone had been disconnected for non-payment and convinced her that Larkin had probably been trying to reach her but that he wouldn't have had any way of knowing that the baby had been delivered early by c-section. I paid the telephone bill and had it turned back on.

When Maria and the baby were released from the hospital a week later, I offered to stay with her until we could locate Larkin. I had just dozed off on the couch in their apartment that night when I heard a key turning in the lock on the front door. It was Larkin. He was as surprised to see me as I was to see him. Maria was asleep in the bedroom. I told him she had given birth to a baby boy prematurely, and explained the circumstances of my coming to Rio. He didn't respond in any way except to go into the kitchen and pour himself a drink. I could have used one myself, but he didn't offer and I didn't ask. When he came back into the living room he began to explain his absence during Maria's travails, but he never looked at me. It was as if he were talking out loud to himself and I just happened to be in the room.

"A partially completed film is as worthless as tits on a boar," he said, pacing back and forth. "I had to find the money to finish the film and

Monica had contacts in Germany where she thought we might raise it. I used my credit card to buy our tickets and called Maria from the airport to tell her I was leaving, but she didn't answer the phone. I tried a couple of times and then they called the flight. When I got to Berlin I called again and was told that the phone had been disconnected. Then I spoke with the landlord who said he hadn't seen Maria at the apartment for a week. I assumed she was pissed at me and had flown back to the States."

"He didn't tell you Maria had been taken to the hospital?" I asked, unwilling to forgive him so easily.

"Absolutely not! Do you think I wouldn't have immediately returned if I had known what was happening?" he demanded testily.

"Frankly, I don't know what to think. All I know is what I have told you, and it seems to me . . . "

"You know, McShane, I don't give a shit how it seems to you," he countered, raising his voice. "I'm telling you how it was. I assumed Maria had taken off back to the States to have the baby, which was her plan all along. You can believe it or not, I don't much give a damn." Before I had a chance to answer, he added. "And what the hell are you doing here now anyway?" he demanded.

"Nothing much," I said beginning to lose it myself. "Trying to take care of your wife and baby, paying her medical bills and your back rent so she had a place to stay when she got out of the hospital . . . so just write me a check for three grand and I'll be on my way. As a matter of fact, you better make that cash, your checks aren't too good around here."

"You son of a bitch!" Larkin roared, raising his fist.

"Larkin!" Maria screamed. She stood leaning against the bedroom door looking like a witch with her black hair all tangled and her stark white face contorted with rage. "Get out," she hissed.

"I ain't going nowhere, baby. Just settle down."

"We don't need you here. Go back to Monica and sing 'Deutschland Über Alles' to each other in the shower, why don't you?" Maria turned and marched back into the bedroom, slamming the door behind her. He tried to follow her but she locked herself in the bedroom. He pounded on the door. They were cursing each other. It was deja vu except this time it wasn't me pounding on the bedroom door. I picked up my bag and checked out.

When I called the next morning Maria told me that she and Larkin had argued all night long and that he had finally cleared out with no intention of returning. She said she wanted to fly back to Puerto Rico as soon as possible so her mother could help with the baby.

When I arrived at her place shortly after we spoke, she had already started to pack, but she was still very weak from the surgery, and I'm sure the emotional trauma of the breakup with Larkin didn't help matters. I made some coffee while she nursed the baby and then put him in the bassinet to sleep. She looked exhausted and I suggested she take a nap. I offered to keep an eye on the baby. Shortly after she fell asleep, the baby started to cry. I wheeled the bassinet out of the bedroom so he wouldn't awaken Maria. I rocked the bassinet back and forth a few times, but he continued to wail. I finally picked him up and burped him, and he immediately quieted down. I chuckled to myself, because it had been many years since I had performed that task, but I still had the knack. As I started to put him back in the bassinet, I happened to glance at his tiny hands. "My God," I gasped. The thumb and first finger of his left hand were joined together. I stared at my own left hand. The scar from the surgery when they separated my thumb and first finger when I was a baby was still visible, the same as it was with my own father. I quickly counted up the months. It was exactly nine months from my sixty-fifth birthday to the day this baby, my new son, was born.

Chapter Thirteen

It WAS ELEVEN O'CLOCK WHEN Lucette finally called.

"Good morning, Michael. How about inviting me to lunch? Martha tells me there is a delightful restaurant at the top of Snake Mountain. What do you say?"

"I say it sounds like a great idea, and in fact if you insist I'll bring along a story I wrote in which Snake Mountain plays a very important role."

"Great. I'll meet you there at one o'clock. Is that okay?"

"Perfect. Incidentally did you happen to, ah . . ."

"Yes I did," she laughed. "We can talk about it at lunch. Bye."

"Patience, patience," Michael said as he hung up the phone.

Michael arrived a few minutes early and parked in front of the lookout beside the restaurant. It was a clear crisp day with a brisk wind blowing at the top of the mountain. When Lucette parked beside him, he opened her car door and escorted her over to the observation deck and demanded that she look through the telescope.

"Do you mind telling me what this is all about," she said laughing.

"You'll understand when you read my story *Smitty's.*"

"The view is spectacular!" she cried. "What does it have to do with your story?"

"You'll see. How did you like the drive up the mountain?"

"If you must know, it scared me to death. And I'm not a sissy when it comes to driving in the mountains in winter. I'm a Colorado girl, you know, but Snake Mountain is properly named for sure." He put his arm around her to shield her from the wind and they scurried into the restaurant. It was warm and cozy inside, and they were quickly seated at a table for two looking out over the surrounding valley.

"Beats Central Park but not Colorado," she jibed.

"I'm willing to call it a tie to avoid a knock-down, drag-out battle so early in the day," he countered.

After they ordered, Michael waited patiently to learn what she thought about his writing. Finally she reached over and took his hand in hers. "I have good news and bad news. Which do you want to hear first?" she asked.

"Well," he said, bringing her fingertips up to his lips, "since I don't ever want to discuss any kind of unhappiness while we are together, I'm going to opt for the good news first and hope the bad news goes away while we are celebrating the good news. Okay?"

"Spoken like a true optimist. The problem is I am a scientist, a realist, I only venture into the world of fantasy when I go to the theater or the cinema or . . ."she smiled, "when I read a good story, which brings me to the best news. I enjoyed *Flesh of my Flesh*. I have some questions to ask you about it and perhaps a suggestion or two for you to consider."

"What a relief," Michael said, dramatically wiping his brow with his napkin, "I thought that was going to be the bad news. I was sure you were going to tell me you hated it and you brought me up here so I could jump off a cliff."

"I do believe your ego bruises easily, Mr. O'Leary, but I have known that since the moment we met," she smiled, a bit sadly he thought. "Keeping that in mind," she continued, "is your story wholly fiction or are there pieces of Michael O'Leary lurking in there?"

"I think it is almost impossible to write fiction without allowing your own experiences to creep in once in a while. What does your sister say?"

"She claims all her sex scenes are nonfiction," she laughed.

"Now you must tell me her name so I can run right out and buy her books. I read three or four novels a week and devour the *Sunday Times Book Review* religiously. Perhaps I've already read something she has written."

"She writes under the name Francine Hart. Does that ring a bell?"

"No, but she probably hasn't heard of me either," he chuckled.

"I want you to meet her. You know she's here visiting Martha as well. It's the first time we have all been together at Christmas for a very long time, and it is wonderful."

"So what suggestions do you have to improve my story?" Michael asked.

"Well for one thing, I wonder if it's fair to leave me hanging in midair at the end. Do Paul and Maria reconcile and live happily ever after in sunny California, or does he wash his hands of her and the baby and return to Erin's welcoming arms?"

"How would you like it to end?" he asked.

"I'm not sure, but wouldn't it be wonderful if we could rearrange our own lives as easily as the fiction writer can change the lives of his characters. Your story can have a happy or sad ending at your whim, with a stroke of your pen, but in the real world . . ." she sighed.

"What about *our* story. You and me in the real world. Will you let me write the next chapter?" he asked, pouring the last bit of their second bottle of wine into her glass.

"No, but I would be very interested in reading the first draft."

"All right, let me think a moment." Michael looked at his watch. "Good Lord. Can you believe we've been gabbing away here for almost five hours? The sun is below the yard arm. It's happy hour. What would you like to drink?"

"If I have one more drink you'll have to carry me home and put me to bed."

"Promise? . . . Waiter, bring the lady another drink."

"That's typical male strategy. Get 'em drunk so they can't resist. Don't bother to charm them, just get 'em pie-eyed."

"It's never failed me before. Besides, I have succeeded in staving off the bad news for over five hours. Did it disappear, I hope?"

"Maybe," she replied hesitantly.

"Great, now where were we? Oh, I remember, in the next chapter I carry you home and take you to bed, and . . ."

"Michael, be serious for a minute. I have something important to tell you. This little romantic holiday adventure of ours is getting out of hand, at least for me. I think we should slow things down. I was going to suggest that we not see each other for a little while so that I could get my priorities straight, but . . . I don't seem to have what it takes to do that now. I'm thirty-seven years old and I'm acting like a teenager."

"If you think for a moment that I will let you cool down this affair, you are sadly mistaken."

"Listen, Counselor, if I decide to go into hibernation what do you think you could do about it?"

"I'd huff and I'd puff and I'd blow your house down."

"I don't live in a straw house, Michael, and I think it's time for me to take off my magic slippers and start thinking like a biochemist again. Please order me some strong coffee because I'm going to drive home right now, and I don't want to see you or talk to you until our dinner date Christmas Eve."

The Fleming sisters were seated around the kitchen table in assorted states of deshabille. The aroma of fresh strudel filled the room.

Martha Fleming Wharton lit a cigarette, blew the smoke toward the ceiling and sipped her coffee.

"When are you going to quit smoking, Martha? I would like to have you around for a while," Lucette pleaded.

"My house, my life," Martha quipped.

"I guess I can't quarrel with that," Lucette sighed, shrugging her shoulders.

"So what is planned for this evening?" the youngest sister, nicknamed Sissy, asked, changing the subject before Lucette and Martha went at each other again on the evils and virtues of smoking.

"If I told you I had a date tonight would you all be upset with me?" Lucette asked hesitantly."

"It's Christmas Eve for God's sake," Martha snapped.

"I know, and it's not that I don't love you guys, it's only that he seems to be a very nice man and I think I could like him . . . a lot, and he seems to like me and now I'm feeling guilty about agreeing to see him tonight," Lucette said sorrowfully.

"Well don't," Sissy exclaimed, biting into another piece of warm strudel. "I think it's great. You've been moping around since your divorce, and I, for one, think it's high time you got back into circulation. Why should you stay home on Christmas Eve and play a hot game of Scrabble with your sisters and your brother-in-law when you could be out swinging with Mr. Right? Who is he anyway?"

"He's a mediocre lawyer who plays a fair game of tennis, is a terrible pool player and writes short stories," Lucette laughed.

"Sounds wonderful. Just like my Ben, except Ben doesn't practice law, play tennis, shoot pool or write short stories. But he's mediocre in everything else."

Sissy started to giggle and then they all started and couldn't stop. When they finally settled down and more fresh coffee was poured all around, Sissy spoke up. "How about a compromise, Luce? Why not bring Mr. Right by the house here for drinks before you go off on your date so we can all get a look at him?"

"Sounds fair to me," Martha chimed in. "What's Romeo's name anyway?"

"Michael O'Leary," Lucette replied.

"Michael O'Leary!" Sissy exclaimed. "Well I think he's nice too, and if he weren't too old for me I'd give you a run for your money," Sissy grinned.

"Wait a minute, Sissy, how come you know Michael?"

"Very simple. I've started another novel in which there is a beautiful lady who is plotting the demise of her husband. I went to the library to do some research on the law involved, but they didn't have what I wanted. On the way home I walked past Mr. O'Leary's law office, and decided on the spur of the moment to pop in and see if he could help me. I thought maybe if I smiled sweetly he wouldn't charge me, but he did. Of course, now that he is my big sister's boyfriend, I'll be able to get all the information I need for free."

Martha called Michael and invited him to come by for some Christmas cheer before taking Lucette out for the evening. He readily agreed and showed up with a bottle of chilled Champagne. When he met Rhonda Fleming for the second time and learned that she wasn't planning to kill anyone except on page twenty-three of her new book he felt greatly relieved.

"You probably won't believe this, Ms. Fleming, but I have been reading the obituaries every day since you left my office, praying that I wouldn't find a report of the death of a Mr. Fleming. What a relief," he exclaimed. "Wait until I tell Doc that the story has a happy ending. He loves stories with happy endings."

"So do I," the three sisters sang out.

"Well, then," Michael said eagerly, "let me tell you about the story I'm working on right now." He took a large swallow of his Champagne, stood up and began to pace nervously in front of the assembled group as if he were addressing a jury, which in a way he was.

"First of all, Rhonda, you have to promise me you won't steal my plot for your new book."

"Only if you give me back my twenty-five bucks," she said with a straight face. Michael groaned, reached in his pocket, took out a handful of bills, studied them carefully, put them back in his pocket and said, "Never mind, you can use my plot if you want to."

"Okay, it goes like this," he continued. "You see, there is this mediocre lawyer who meets this gorgeous, very bright, principled lady at a party. So he makes a stupid, insensitive remark and the lady immediately puts him down, cuts him right off at the knees. Now, deep down, this character is a pretty decent guy and he wants to redeem himself in her eyes. So he invites her to have lunch with him on the top of Hogback Mountain where this genius introduces her to one of his male friends who is young, ruggedly handsome, witty, and available."

"Hold it, hold it. Forget the twenty-five bucks, just introduce me to your friend," Sissy giggled.

"I don't think you people are taking this whole thing seriously," Michael complained.

"No, no," everyone protested. "We are . . . more, more," Martha applauded.

"Okay, if you all insist," he continued. "Fortunately, our heroine, being the lady she is, remains loyal to the mediocre lawyer and does not take up residence with the handsome forest ranger, and agrees to have dinner with the lawyer and his best friends. Now listen carefully," Michael admonished them, "because we are coming to the good part." Everyone leaned forward in mock rapture. "Well, at some point during the evening of the dinner party after his best friends leave, and the mediocre lawyer and the lovely lady have finished doing the dishes and discussed their hopes and aspirations for the balance of their lives, the mediocre lawyer thought he might be falling for the lovely lady. Then when he held her close while they danced to old Bing singing "White Christmas," he was pretty certain he was falling for her. And after she left, he sat in his big old armchair in front of the fire until the wee hours of the morning, thinking about her and the effect she was having upon him, and trying to understand what it all meant. Then they met the next day and as soon as he saw her he knew he no longer had a choice. So if the lovely lady's sisters will forgive her for abandoning them on Christmas Eve, the mediocre lawyer is planning to ask the lovely lady a very important question during dinner."

"Oh dear," Martha said, misty eyed, "I love a story with a happy ending."

Acknowledgment

But for a chance meeting at the local library with Susan Shefter, my short stories would have languished, turning to dust in the upstairs closet underneath discarded hockey sticks and umbrellas in need of repair. On that fateful day Ms. Shefter, a freelance editor, offered to read my stories. With her encouragement, professional eye and critical red pen, *Willow Run* became a reality. I shall be ever grateful to her for her friendship and support.